RETHINKING THE GOSPEL

CHALLENGING THE MODERN MISCONCEPTION

KEVIN SIMINGTON

SFP

CONTENTS

❀ Created with Vellum

PART I

THE MISSING ELEMENT

THE GOSPEL WE KNOW

There is a crucial element of the gospel that has been largely de-emphasised and, in some cases, almost completely ignored since the start of the Reformation in the 1500s. In many churches today, this aspect of the gospel is largely missing from public preaching, and its absence has had a significant impact upon the kind of disciples that the modern church is producing.

But before we launch into this important topic, let me begin by describing the aspect of the gospel that *is* well understood. In this first chapter, I want to explain, as clearly as I can, the free and undeserved nature of grace along with its absolute necessity as the only means of salvation.

We are saved by grace, and grace alone. This is the golden mantra of Christianity. Ask any Bible-believing Christian and they will tell you that salvation is by grace from beginning to end. Our own good works cannot save us. Nothing we do can merit salvation. No amount of good deeds can bring us to a point where we earn or deserve a place in God's eternal kingdom. This is because any good deeds that we manage to perform cannot atone for the huge weight of sin that we accumulate over our lifetime. Even the most righteous among us is hopelessly short of God's perfect standards.

You see, the gospel actually starts with very bad news. The scriptures teach us that we are all born with a sinful nature that leads us consistently and inexorably toward disobedience and rebellion against God's perfect moral code:

"Surely I was sinful at birth, sinful from the time my mother conceived me" (Psalm 51:5)

The extent and depth of our sin is no trivial thing. The Bible's testimony is clear. We are not basically good people who make occasional moral blunders: we are consumed and controlled by our sinful natures. We are sinful at the very core of our being, and out of that core flows a daily stream of individual sin: lust, greed, selfishness, pride, hatred, judgmentalism, unforgiveness, jealousy, slander, lies, gossip, cheating, stealing. And that's just Monday mornings! Then on Monday afternoons ...

Our sins accumulate on a daily basis. A selfish action. A lustful thought. A proud attitude. A cutting remark. An act of unforgiveness. A smutty joke. A distortion of the truth. An act of deception. A judgmental attitude. A cruel word of gossip. A derisory put-down. A snide comment. Lying to cover up for our mistakes. Cheating our employer by not working hard enough or taking longer breaks than we are entitled to. Failing to love and respect someone as they deserve. Failing to help someone in need (as Jesus defined sin in Matthew 25). The list is almost endless.

Most of us would easily clock up at least three sins each day. Over the course of an average lifetime, that amounts to about 70,000 sins! This is why anyone claiming to have *"lived a good life"* is only fooling themselves.

Imagine a criminal who has committed 70,000 crimes, standing in the dock of a courtroom. The evidence is presented to the judge, and it is unequivocal. The man really has committed 70,000 crimes! The judge then asks him, *"Before I pass sentence, do you have anything to say for yourself?"* Incredibly, the criminal sticks out his chest, looks the judge in the eye and says, *"Your honour, I've lived a good life."* It would be an utterly ridiculous claim for him to make, wouldn't it? He would be laughed out of court. Yet this is the foolish claim that many people make in regard to their own self-perceived righteousness. Despite having committed tens of thousands of sins over their lifetime, repeatedly and blatantly breaking God's commandments, they naïvely insist that they have lived a good life.

If you are in any doubt as to your own complete sinfulness and your desperate standing before your Creator, a quick read of these verses will set you straight:

"The Lord saw how great man's wickedness on the earth had become, and that every inclination of the thoughts of their heart was only evil all the time." (Genesis 6:5)

"There is no one on earth who is righteous, no one who does what is right and never sins." (Ecclesiastes 7:20)

"There is no one who understands, no one who seeks God. All have turned away; they have together become worthless; there is no one who does good, not even one. Their throats are open graves; their

tongues practice deceit. The venom of vipers is on their lips. Their mouths are full of cursing and bitterness. Their feet are swift to shed blood; ruin and misery mark their ways, and the way of peace they do not know. There is no fear of God before their eyes." (Romans 3:11-18)

"We all, like sheep, have gone astray, each of us has turned to our own way." (Isaiah 53:6 and 1 Peter 2:25)

"All have sinned, and fall short of the glory of God." (Romans 3:23)

The Bible is unequivocal: our souls are not predominantly white with a few specs of sin that our benign Creator will somehow overlook. They are stained black with the huge and dreadful record of our daily wrong-doing, irrevocably etched into the very essence of our being. We are not good people who make occasional moral blunders: we are bad people who do occasional good things, but even then, our good works are often tainted with pride and selfish motives. Such is the depth of our sinfulness.

Our complete inability to overcome this pervasive sinful nature means that we are utterly unable to save ourselves. There is nothing we can do to atone for the huge weight of our wrong-doing or somehow expunge its record from our souls. Any person who thinks they will be able to stand in God's presence on the Day of Judgment and claim to have *"lived a good life"* – to have perfectly obeyed all his commandments – is completely deluded.

"Every mouth will be silenced and the whole world held accountable to God. Therefore, no one will be declared righteous in God's sight by

the works of the law; rather, through the law we become conscious of sin." (Romans 3:19-20)

The ultimate consequence of our pervasive sinfulness, this vast record of our wrongdoing, is separation from God, both now and forever:

"Your iniquities have separated you from your God; your sins have hidden his face from you so that he will not hear." (Isaiah 59:2)

"For the wages of sin is death." (Romans 6:23)

"... and they will go away to eternal punishment." (Matthew 25:46)

That is the bad news of the gospel. Our sins have cut us off from God eternally and there is nothing we can do about it. The weight of our sin is so overwhelming, the record of our wrong-doing is so vast and extensive, that no amount of good deeds can take it away. We may regularly help little old ladies across the road, give to charity, volunteer for meals-on-wheels, or even don ministerial robes and serve at the church altar on a Sunday, but none of these things have the power to undo or expunge the vast and growing weight of sin that accumulates within our souls on a daily basis. We are unable to save ourselves. Our constant and pervasive sin has separated us from God and we are completely unable to make amends.

But God has not left us in this state. He has provided a remedy. The death of the Son of God, Jesus Christ, on a cruel Roman cross 2,000 years ago was not an unfortunate end to an otherwise promising life. It was the primary purpose of Jesus' visit to our planet. He came to die a substitutionary death, allowing himself to be punished in our place, suffering the full wrath of God's punishment for the sins of the whole world, so that God's justice could be satisfied and we could walk free. Mankind was on death row, pronounced guilty, sentenced to death and awaiting final execution, when the Son of God stepped in and died in our place. He took the punishment that we deserved, so that we could be forgiven. Somehow, by means of a spiritual transaction, the exact nature of which we can only dimly perceive, the death of Christ on the cross and his resurrection from the dead paid for the sins of the whole world.

"He is the atoning sacrifice for our sins, and not only for ours but also for the sins of the whole world." (1 John 2:2)

As he hung on the cross, dying, God the Father punished God the Son, the innocent one, for every sin that ever has been committed and ever will be committed.

"We all like sheep have gone astray, each of us has turned to our own way, but the Lord laid on him the iniquity of us all." (Isaiah 53:6)

"He himself bore our sins in his body on the cross." (1 Peter 2:24)

The extent of the punishment that Christ endured on the cross cannot be underestimated. We will never fully understand the depth of his suffering – spiritual and physical – but there are glimpses of it in the descriptions of that terrible event, provided for us by the gospel writers. Matthew, Mark and Luke record Jesus' terror on the eve of his impending crucifixion, as he prayed in the garden of Gethsemane, asking the Father if there was any possible way of avoiding the horrendous events of the next day.

" 'Father, if you are willing, take this cup from me; yet not my will but yours be done.' An angel from heaven appeared to him and strengthened him. And being in anguish, he prayed more earnestly,

and his sweat was like drops of blood falling to the ground." (Luke 22:42-44)

Furthermore, Matthew and Mark record the anguished cry of Jesus as he hung, dying on the cross.

"My God, my God, why have you forsaken me?" (Matthew 27:46 and Mark 15:34)

We need to interpret this cry of Jesus literally. As Jesus hung on the cross, he was, for the first time in eternity, utterly cut off from God the Father. God was punishing Jesus as if he had committed every sin in the world. Jesus was experiencing the full wrath of God against every act of evil that has ever been and ever will be committed. The full fury of God was being poured out upon him: the righteous anger of a holy and just God against every act of injustice and depravity and hatred and selfishness that humankind has ever committed.

As a sign of the terrible spiritual punishment that Jesus was enduring, three of the Gospel writers, Matthew, Mark and Luke, record the fact that a supernatural darkness came over the land during the crucifixion.

"It was now about noon, and darkness came over the whole land until three in the afternoon, for the sun had stopped shining." (Luke 23:44-45)

Matthew records other extraordinary signs that took place as Jesus took his final breath:

"At that moment the curtain of the temple was torn in two from top to bottom. The earth shook, the rocks split and the tombs broke open. The bodies of many holy people who had died were raised to life.

They came out of the tombs after Jesus' resurrection and went into the holy city and appeared to many people." (Matthew 27:51-53).

Significantly, Thallus, a first century Greek historian, also wrote of this supernatural darkness and the earthquake that accompanied Christ's crucifixion. His reference was later quoted by the second century Roman historian, Sextus Julius Africanus:

"On the whole world there pressed a fearful darkness, and the rocks were rent by an earthquake, and many places in Judea and other districts were thrown down. Thallus calls this darkness an eclipse of the sun in the third book of histories, without reason it seems to me."

These astounding astronomical and geological phenomena at the time of Jesus' crucifixion signify the dreadful events that were taking place in the spiritual realm. Matthew records the fact that the people surrounding the cross who witnessed these events were *"terrified"* (Matthew 27:54). God's justice was being satisfied, judicial sentence was being carried out, sin was being punished, and the physical manifestations of that awful reality were enough to cause the first-century onlookers to step back in terror.

This substitutionary death of Christ for mankind is the pivotal point of human history. It is the point to which all previous history was leading and the point from which all subsequent history derives its meaning. In fact, it was God's grand plan from the beginning of eternity to send Christ to the cross in order to rescue and redeem fallen humanity. Speaking of this eternal plan of salvation, the Apostle Peter writes:

"You were redeemed by the precious blood of Christ, a lamb without

blemish or defect. <u>He was chosen before the creation of the world</u> and was revealed in these last times for your sake." (1 Peter 1:19-20)

The result of this extraordinary sacrificial act is the possibility of a new legal status before God for anyone who wishes it. The way has now been cleared for us to be reconciled to God. God's justice has been satisfied. The judicial sentence has been carried out. The penalty for our sins has been paid in full. Indeed, this is indicated by Christ's last word, as he took his final breath on the cross: *"tetelestai" - "paid in full"* – recorded in John 19:30 (and sometimes also translated *"nothing more to pay"* and *"it is finished"* in various translations). Christ's resurrection from the dead on the following Sunday morning was the ultimate proof that our debt had been paid in full and that the way back to God was now open. Christ's crucifixion was the payment for our sin and his resurrection was the official receipt, proving that his payment was complete and sufficient. It also proves that he was who he claimed to be; the eternal Son of God. Because of Christ's sacrifice, the way is now opened for mankind to be reconciled to God:

"Christ died for sins, once for all, the righteous for the unrighteous, <u>to bring you to God</u>." (1 Peter 3:18)

This is a truly stunning development. The criminal awaiting execution on death row has received an eleventh-hour pardon. Someone else has stepped in and been executed in his place. His debt has been paid, the prison cell door has been opened and he is free to go. This does not mean that this allegorical criminal is innocent. He is not. He is still guilty of the crimes he committed. But he has been pardoned. Someone else has paid for his crimes. And because of that, his death sentence has been remitted. He is set free and will henceforth be *treated* as if he is not guilty. This is what theologians refer to as *imputed righteousness*. Even though the criminal is guilty of crime, he is now *treated* as if he had never committed them. He is free to re-enter society and enjoy all the benefits of unfettered citizenship.

This is the allegory that the Bible uses to describe the new legal standing before God that all in Christ have been granted. Our sins are paid for. Our condemnation has been removed. We have been set free to live in relationship with God as he intended.

"Therefore, there is now no condemnation for those who are in Christ Jesus, because through Christ Jesus the law of the Spirit who gives life has set you free from the law of sin and death. For what the law was powerless to do because it was weakened by the flesh, God did by sending his own Son in the likeness of sinful flesh to be a sin offering. And so he condemned sin in the flesh." (Romans 8:1-3)

The stunning result of Christ's sacrificial death on the cross and his resurrection from the dead is that every human being is now offered a *free* pardon.

"The wages of sin is death, but the free gift of God is eternal life through Christ Jesus our Lord." (Romans 6:23)

This is the good news of the gospel. In fact, it is not just good news: it is great news! It is stupendous news! It is the best news possible! The way to heaven stands open and free entry is granted to anyone who desires it. Your past can be wiped clean. A free pardon is yours for the taking.

This is what is meant by the gospel of *grace*. Salvation is not a matter of earning our way into God's favour, because that is demonstrably impossible. No one will be saved on their own merits. Salvation is only possible on the merits of Christ – what he has achieved for us through his sacrifice on the cross. Salvation is a free, unmerited gift from an unimaginably generous benefactor. Salvation is by grace, and grace alone, and not through any works of our own.

"For all have sinned and fall short of the glory of God, and are justified freely by his grace through the redemption that came by Jesus Christ." (Romans 3:23-24)

But it is an offer only. Christ's sacrifice on the cross does us no good at all unless and until we accept it and receive it for ourselves. The forgiveness that Christ purchased on the cross is not automatically transferred to everyone. It must be intentionally *received*.

"God presented Christ as a sacrifice of atonement, through the shedding of his blood, to be received by faith." (Romans 3:25)

Let us revisit the allegorical condemned criminal on death row. Christ opens the cell door, walks in and offers the criminal a free pardon, signed by God himself. All the criminal needs to do is humble himself and receive it with a grateful, penitent heart, resolving to live a new, reformed life with the freedom he is being offered. He simply needs to reach out and receive the free pardon. It would be utterly foolish for him to reject it, would it not? Yet this is what many people do.

Two centuries ago, there was an extraordinary case of a man who literally refused a death row pardon. In 1833, George Wilson was convicted of robbing the U.S. Mail in Pennsylvania and was sentenced to death. His many friends advocated for him and petitioned the government. Finally, President Andrew Jackson granted Wilson a presidential pardon. However, in an unprecedented and extraordinary turn of events, George Wilson refused to accept the pardon. His guards and friends and legal councillors all pleaded with him, showing him the signed presidential pardon, to no avail. Wilson was adamant that he did not want to be pardoned. This unprecedented situation created much confusion within the legal system. No one knew what to do. Eventually, the case was taken to the Supreme Court which, after much deliberation, delivered the following verdict:

"A pardon is a deed, to the validity of which delivery is essential, and delivery is not complete without acceptance. It may then be rejected by the person to whom it is tendered; and if it is rejected, we have discovered no power in this court to force it upon him." (https://supreme.justia.com/cases/federal/us/32/150/)

In other words, *a pardon is only valid if it is accepted*. George Wilson was eventually hanged, simply because of his obstinate refusal to accept a free pardon.

As difficult to believe as that example is (and I assure you, it is factual), this is precisely what is occurring all over our world today in regard to Christ's offer of salvation. The penalty for sin has been paid and a free pardon is held out to all mankind. Christ stands at the door to our prison cell and holds out a pardon written in his blood and signed by his Father. All we need to do is accept the free gift, by accepting the giver himself – Jesus Christ, our Lord and Saviour. But, tragically, almost unbelievably, many people refuse. And because they refuse, the pardon is forfeited and their sentence must be carried out, just as it was in the case of George Wilson.

Why would anyone reject Christ's offer of a free pardon? There are really only two reasons: pride and unbelief. The proud are convinced that they can do it themselves. *"I've lived a good life. I'm a good person. I've done enough for God to let me into heaven."* Such a person has no comprehension of the depth of their own sinfulness and how impossibly short of God's standards they fall. I remember a conversation I once had with a woman immediately after a sermon that I had preached on this very topic. The conversation went roughly as follows:

Woman: "I don't need God's grace. I've never really sinned."

Me: "Really? What about the 10 commandments?"

Woman: "I've kept all of them."

Me: "Really? What about the first two. They talk about placing God before anything or anyone else in your life. Can you honestly say you've done that?"

Woman: "Well, not those two, but I've kept all the others."

Me: "OK. What about the next one: don't misuse the name of God. Have you ever used God's name as a swear word?"

Woman: "Yes, I suppose so."

Me: "So not that commandment either? OK. What about the next one: remember the sabbath day and keep it holy. Have you diligently kept aside one day of the week to solely worship and honour God?"

Woman: "No. I guess not."

I continued with the rest of the commandments that talk about our need to honour our parents, to not murder (redefined by Jesus as hating others), to not commit adultery (redefined by Jesus a looking lustfully at others), to not steal, to not lie and to not covet the possessions of others. At the end of our discussion the woman admitted that she scored zero out of ten! Sadly, she still refused to accept her need for a saviour because she still saw herself as much better than most people. Her problem was that she was comparing herself to others, instead of comparing herself to the Holy God and his perfect standards. Pride gives people an inflated sense of their own goodness and stops them from seeing how desperately in need of forgiveness they are.

Unbelief is the other reason people refuse Christ's offer of salvation. They don't believe that Jesus is who he said he was - the Son of God, the Lord of mankind and the saviour of the world. They refuse to believe the overwhelming evidence of his miracles, as recorded by verifiable historical documents. They refuse to believe that there is anything beyond the grave. They refuse to accept the message of the Bible and choose, instead, to believe in the myth of a godless universe and a meaningless existence. The Apostle John refers to this kind of unbelief as the key factor that will ultimately separate people from God:

"Whoever believes in the Son has eternal life. But whoever rejects the Son will not see life, for God's wrath remains on them." (John 3:36)

The sad fact is that there will be many people who end up separated from God eternally, experiencing his wrath for their sins, not because they are worse sinners that you or I, but simply because of their pride and unbelief.

In many ways, the gospel of grace is difficult to believe. It seems too good to be true, doesn't it? It seems too simple. Surely it can't be that easy? Surely there must be more that I must do? The Apostle Paul describes the gospel of grace as a seemingly foolish message:

"For the message of the cross is foolishness to those who are perishing, but to us who are being saved it is the power of God." (1 Corinthians 1:18)

The gospel of grace seems a foolish message because it completely undercuts our desire to be self-sufficient, to be self-achievers, to see ourselves as more worthy than others and to attain our own salvation through the merits of our own good living. It cuts us all down to the same level. It declares that we are all hopeless sinners, equally in need of mercy and equally unable to save ourselves. It depicts us all as helpless beggars before a holy and almighty God.

It takes a certain degree of humility to accept that diagnosis and receive God's pardon. In fact, humility is an essential ingredient in order to be saved.

"God opposes the proud, but gives grace to the humble." (James 4:6)

The kind of humility that is required in order to receive God's grace is the humility shown by the repentant criminal who was crucified beside Jesus. The Gospel writers record two criminals who were crucified alongside Jesus on the hill called Golgotha and records their two very different responses to Jesus. Their responses are an allegory of the two distinct responses toward Jesus that people continue to make today. One criminal demonstrated unbelief and pride, hurling insults at Jesus and ridiculing him, refusing to believe that he was who he claimed to be. The other criminal responded very differently. He began by rebuking the first criminal:

"Don't you fear God, since we are under the same sentence? We are punished justly, for we are getting what our sins deserve, but this man has done nothing wrong." (Luke 23:40-41).

This is a frank admission. He must have done some very bad things if he admits that both he and the other criminal deserve to die. Make no mistake about it, these two criminals were very bad people! But then this second criminal turned to Jesus and responded completely unexpectedly:

"Jesus, remember me when you come into your kingdom." (Luke 23:42)

In responding as he did, this second criminal expressed a simple faith in Jesus as the coming King, admitted his own guilt and asked for mercy. Then we come to the most surprising, indeed shocking, part of this whole incident. To this second criminal, Jesus responded:

"Truly, I say to you, today you will be with me in paradise." (Luke 23:43)

What an astonishing statement! Jesus was effectively saying that this self-confessed criminal, who by his own admission had committed such serious crimes that he deserved to die, would be granted a free pass into heaven! How could Jesus allow such a self-confessed baddie into God's paradise? How could Jesus overlook the terrible things that this man must have done? The answer is that Jesus *didn't* overlook this man's sin. Instead, he paid the price for it himself. Even as they were having that conversation, Jesus was dying for that man's sin. He was paying the penalty for that man's wrong-doing, so that people like him, and people like me and you, can be forgiven.

And did you notice what that forgiven criminal did NOT have a chance to do? He didn't have a chance to turn over a new leaf. He didn't have a chance to lift his game, to clean up his act, to stop doing bad things and to make himself more acceptable to God. All he could do was continue to hang there, dying. He was not able to offer up a SINGLE THING toward his own salvation. He could only do one thing, the only thing that any of us can do: he threw himself on the mercy of Jesus, acknowledging Jesus as his rightful King and trusting in Jesus for his forgiveness. That's it! Nothing else! And that is precisely what everyone must do in order to be saved.

You see, salvation is all about God's grace, freely given, undeserved and unmerited. We bring nothing to the table. Our hands are empty. In fact, they must be empty. It is only when they are empty that we can reach out and receive. They must be empty of any and all things that we would hold up to God, saying *"Look what I have done! Look how good I am! Look at my achievements! Look at my good life! Surely I deserve eternal life!"* God turns aside from people with full hands and proud hearts, for he sees their achievements for what they are: pitifully inadequate offerings, tainted by pride and completely inadequate in their inability to atone for the vast record of their sinfulness.

"For it is by grace you are saved, through faith, and this not from yourselves, it is the gift of God, not by works, so that no one can boast." (Ephesians 2:8-9)

This is the biblical doctrine of grace. It is the precious heart of the gospel and the gleaming jewel at the centre of the Bible's narrative. It is the thing that sets Christianity apart from all other religions. Every other religion in the world proposes a path whereby a person can strive to achieve a level of enlightenment or purity or moral integrity or personal piety in order to ultimately attain some kind of salvation. The Bible proclaims that this is a lost cause because no amount of self-actualisation or self-improvement can save us from our own sinful nature. We can't pull ourselves up by our own boot laces. We need a saviour. And Jesus is that saviour: attested by miracles, affirmed by his extraordinary teaching and ultimately validated by his resurrection from the dead.

We are saved by grace, through faith in Jesus, our Saviour and Lord.

This is the truth upon which Bible-believing Christians stand. It is the promise upon which our faith rests and our hope is founded. It is the message that we cherish and proclaim.

So, in this very first chapter, before we go on to explore some of the other elements of the gospel, let me pause and ask you: have you properly understood and received this grace for yourself? It is entirely possible, indeed it is sadly very common, for a person to be deeply religious and have never truly understood and received the grace of Jesus. It is possible to believe in God and even be deeply committed to religious worship and service, and never receive the grace of Jesus personally. This was the problem with the Pharisees at the time of Jesus. They believed in God. They were committed to worshipping and serving God. They spent their lives studying God's laws. They were dedicated to meticulously defining and teaching God's laws. They were utterly devoted to the pursuit of personal holiness. They tried to follow God's laws to the letter. They even tithed every tenth leaf from their herb gardens! If anyone was going to make it into heaven on their own efforts it was going to be them!

But Jesus described them as "whitewashed tombs" (Matthew 23:27); seemingly squeaky-clean on the outside, but full of death on the inside. In other words, their outward religious observance could not expunge the blackness of the sin that they carried around in their souls. No amount of good works can. The Pharisees were trusting in their own good works, but that trust was totally misplaced. In their ignorance and pride they thought they could save themselves, but they were hopelessly wrong. Only Jesus can save, because only Jesus can wipe away the blackness of our sin. The Apostle Paul writes:

"Therefore no one will be declared righteous in God's sight by the works of the law; rather, through the law we become conscious of our sin." (Romans 3:20)

The Pharisees' meticulous study of God's laws should have made them conscious of their own inadequacy and their desperate need for forgiveness. Instead, they became mistakenly convinced of their own self-righteousness.

What about you? Have you been trusting in your own righteousness? Have you lived your life up until this point under the mistaken belief that if you just do more good works, serve God more faithfully, live life more selflessly, then you will be right with God and he will accept you into his kingdom? If that has been your belief, then you have totally missed the point. You have not understood the depth of your own sinfulness and your powerlessness to expunge its record from your soul. Trying to be justified by your own good works is like sticking bandaids on measles spots: you are trying to cover up the symptoms, but the disease remains untreated. And only Jesus can treat the disease of sin that permeates your soul.

If it is possible for someone to be good enough to earn God's acceptance, then Jesus died in vain. Let me say that again. If it is possible for someone to live a good enough life to be acceptable to God, then Jesus did not have to go to the cross: his death on the cross would not have been necessary.

But it WAS necessary. The fact that Jesus undertook that most extreme action of dying on the cross, tells me that it was necessary. There was no other way to save us. And no one – not Mother Theresa or Billy Graham – has ever reached a point where they can be saved apart from the grace of Jesus, made possible by his atoning sacrifice. We are all spiritually destitute, infected with a terminal disease, and all we can do is hold out empty hands, asking for mercy.

So, let me ask you again: what about you? What are you holding in your hands? What are you trusting in for your salvation? Are you trusting in your own good works? Are you trusting in the record of your good service; your years of charity work or your dedicated service at the altar of your local church? Is that what is in your hands? Is that what you are holding up to God, saying, "*Look what I have done. Surely, this is good enough?*"

If that is the case, you must empty your hands immediately. Right now. Without another moment's hesitation. Those things cannot save you. Only Jesus can. You need the grace of the

Saviour. But you can't receive his grace while your hands are full of your own self-righteousness. You must lay those things down. You must cease trusting in your own goodness, and trust fully and only in the grace of Jesus. You must reach out with empty hands and a humble, penitent heart, asking for his mercy and trusting in his goodness.

Jesus told a poignant parable that vividly depicts the humble, penitent heart that God requires:

"Two men went up to the temple to pray, one a Pharisee and the other a tax collector. The Pharisee stood up and prayed about himself: 'God, I thank you that I am not like other men—robbers, evildoers, adulterers—or even like this tax collector. I fast twice a week and give a tenth of all I get.' But the tax collector stood at a distance. He would not even look up to heaven, but beat his breast and said, 'God, have mercy on me, a sinner.' I tell you that this man, rather than the other, went home justified before God. For everyone who exalts himself will be humbled, and he who humbles himself will be exalted." (Luke 18:10-14)

Which one of those two petitioners are you? If, up until this moment in your life, you have been like the Pharisee, trusting in your own righteousness, then God is calling you to fall on your knees right now and ask for forgiveness. Ask his forgiveness for your arrogance, for your sinfulness and for your misguided belief in your own goodness. Empty your hands and hold them out to the Saviour in simple repentance and faith. This is the pivotal moment of your life. This is the moment that God has been waiting for – the moment when you lay aside your misplaced trust in yourself and trust solely in him.

If you will do this, if you will kneel alongside that penitent tax collector, if you will bow your head and humble your heart alongside the criminal who was crucified at Jesus' side, then you will receive the same mercy they received. Then, and only then, will you be forgiven. And when you do this, you will receive the same assurance that Jesus gave to those two sinners. As the humble tax collector *"went home justified before God"* *(v.13)*, you too will be finally reconciled to the God who made you. And as the penitent criminal was assured, *"Truly, I say to you, today you will be with me in paradise,"* (Luke 23:43), you too will receive a place in God's kingdom that will endure forever. When you kneel in this way before the Saviour, you kneel as an unworthy sinner, but you rise as a child of God.

"To all who received him, to those who believed in his name, he gave the right to become children of God — children born not of natural descent, nor of human decision or a husband's will, but born of God." *(John 1:12-13)*

If you would like to make this step of repentance and faith, don't put it off. Do it now, while the Spirit of God is working in your heart. Here is a simple prayer you might like to pray:

"Dear God, I confess that I am a sinner who has fallen hopelessly short of your perfect standards. I sin in thought, word and deed, deliberately doing what I know to be wrong and failing to do what I know to be right. Please forgive me, not only for these individual sins, but also for the sin of my self-reliance. Lord Jesus, I believe you are the Son of God. I believe you died on the cross to forgive my sins and rose from the dead to be declared Lord of all. I trust you now as my Saviour and I humbly ask for your mercy. I open my heart to you and ask that you will come into my life, fill me with Your presence, and strengthen me to follow you all the days of my life. Amen."

If you prayed that prayer humbly and sincerely, then you have done all that God requires for you to be forgiven. You are a child of God, who has crossed over from death to life, from condemnation to forgiveness, and there is a place in heaven for you. You have been saved by grace.

"Those who are in Christ are a new creation, the old has gone and the new has come." (2 Corinthians 5:17)

Of course, there is a lot more to being a Christian than merely praying a simple prayer. You have pledged to follow Christ as your new Lord (master), and that pledge must be put into action. Your life is pointing in a new direction, and now you must continue down that path. But you have taken your first step. The prison door has swung wide and you have walked through it, holding onto a free pardon written in the blood of the Saviour. You have been saved by grace, through faith.

In this first chapter, I have explained the wonderful gospel of grace, of which you are, hopefully, a grateful recipient.

But there is an element of the gospel that is often overlooked: which, in fact, is the major point of this book. I believe there is an aspect of the gospel that was lost at the very beginning of the Reformation, the loss of which has had a significant impact on the message that we preach and, consequently, on the kind of disciples that are being produced. It centres around the concept of repentance and is what I refer to as the encumbency of grace. In order to understand what it is and how it was lost, we must firstly go back to the 16th century, to the reforms of a lowly German monk named Martin Luther.

2

THE GOSPEL WE LOST

By the Middle Ages, the worldwide Christian church was in a terrible state. It had become bogged down in superstition, hamstrung by bureaucracy, infected with immorality and rife with corruption. Worst of all, the gospel of grace had been replaced with a reliance upon good works and man-made religious observance. The result was that very few people had any clear understanding of the gospel and the significance of the atoning sacrifice of Christ for the sins of the world. The Christian church was like a tree that had been infected with wood rot and was barely clinging to life.

The start of the rot can arguably be traced back to 312 AD, when the Roman Emperor Constantine, was converted to Christianity. There is some debate as to whether his conversion was genuine or merely a religious whim, but either way, his impact on the subsequent development of Christianity was substantial. A year after his conversion, in 313 AD, he issued the Edict of Milan, which commanded the cessation of persecution of Christians and effectively proclaimed Christianity as the official religion of the Roman empire. Initially, this proclamation was a huge blessing to the Christian church, who could now practise their faith openly and even build places of worship.

Gradually, however, the line between church and state became increasingly muddied. The proclamation of Christianity as the state religion led to its wholesale adoption by a populace who knew very little about it. Priests who had previously worshipped the Roman gods now conducted services to the Emperor's newly proclaimed Christian God, with no understanding of the Bible or the gospel. People transferring to the Emperor's new religion often brought with them many of the superstitious beliefs and practices of their previous religion. Within a few decades the Christian church had become monolithic, bureaucratic and infested with misguided beliefs and practices. The headquarters of the worldwide Christian church was changed from Jerusalem to Rome, and a hierarchical system of priests, cardinals and bishops became entrenched, with the Bishop of Rome being proclaimed as the world leader of the church on Earth.

By the Middle Ages, the gospel of salvation by grace had been almost completely forgotten, buried under the accumulated weight of superstitious beliefs and false doctrines declared by a succession of Popes (the new name for the Bishop of Rome). Apart from a split between the Eastern and Western branches of the church in 1054 AD, there was really only one significant expression of Christianity on Earth. There were no denominations yet, just the official Roman Catholic Church. The word "Roman", referred to its centre of its government, and "Catholic", simply meant "worldwide" or "universal". By the

Middle Ages, the Pope had been decreed to be the infallible representative of God on Earth – decreed by a succession of Popes themselves!

The period from 500 A.D. to 1500 A.D. is known as the Dark Ages of the church. During this period, a cascading litany of doctrinal decrees flowed from the Popes, which moved the church further and further away from the teachings of the Bible. This was made possible by the fact that, by then, very few priests, bishops or cardinals even bothered to read the Bible. Part of the cause of this biblical illiteracy was due to the fact that the Popes had declared that the Bible was too holy to be translated into common languages, and must only be translated into Latin. All other translations were outlawed. Latin was the language of the scholars, and only those who had studied at university could read it. The vast majority of clergy – bishops, priests and Cardinals, had not studied Latin. Most common people were completely illiterate, and those few who could read had certainly never studied Latin. Thus, the vast majority of people, including priests, were unable to read the Bible. This suited the Roman Catholic Church, for a succession of Popes had declared that the Bible was too complex for the average person to understand. Keeping the Bible in Latin was a way of maintaining control over the populace. For this reason, very few priests had ever actually read the Bible and were largely ignorant of its teachings. Priests simply regurgitated the official doctrines of the church that were passed down from the Pope.

Because priestly appointments could be quite lucrative, the priesthood became a popular profession, attracting many people who were unconverted. Consequently, sexual immorality amongst the clergy was rampant. In major cities and towns there were high class brothels that were dedicated to servicing the priests who, according to official church doctrine, were supposed to be celibate. Many priests also set up a woman in lodgings in his town or village and kept her as his unofficial wife. This practice was well-known and silently accepted by the priest's local parishioners, who turned a blind eye to the practice. Even many of the Popes were well-known for having numerous mistresses and children. For example, Wikipedia lists six Popes who fathered illegitimate children, a further eight Popes who had affairs without fathering children, and four Popes who had homosexual affairs.

Furthermore, priests who had ambition, could purchase a better parish for themselves, by paying the Vatican large sums of money. Similarly, priests often ascended the ecclesiastical hierarchy, becoming Bishops and Cardinals, by purchasing these positions from the Vatican.

The official teachings of the Roman Catholic Church during the Middles Ages became polluted with all kinds of medieval superstition. The common people were told that only priests had the power to forgive their sins. Supposed relics of dead saints were said to have magical powers, and the church charged money for people to touch them and worship them. Greed and corruption added further to the polluting of Christian doctrine. Forgiveness of sins was sold for money. People could buy an "indulgence" - an official certificate signed by a bishop or, on special occasions, by the Pope himself, absolving them of their sins. The church also introduced the concept of purgatory, and consequently sold more indulgences, which supposedly enabled people to pay money to free their dead relatives from the flames of torment. One famous priest who was particularly effective in selling these indulgences on behalf of the Pope and various bishops, was Johann Tetzel (1465-1519), who used the catch-cry, *"When a coin in the coffers rings, a soul from purgatory springs"*. Under the Pope's authority he even claimed that an indulgence certificate *"could forgive even someone who has had sex with the virgin Mary herself!"*

The sale of these Indulgences, as well as charges for access to relics, brought huge amounts of money into the coffers of the Roman Catholic church. Sadly, it also completely undermined the gospel of grace. People were taught to trust in superstitious relics, man-made certificates and religious observance for their forgiveness, rather than trusting in Christ. Both priests and laity alike knew no better. Those few individuals who did gain an understanding of the teachings of Christ, and who dared to voice beliefs that differed from the official dogma of the Church were often brought before the Inquisition and charged with heresy.

It was truly a grim, dark period in the Church's history. The institutional Roman Catholic Church was corrupt, superstitious, immoral and controlling. The true Gospel was largely lost, and genuine Christianity among laity and clergy was a rare thing.

This was the world into which Martin Luther was born, in 1483, in Eisleben, Germany. By 1505, Luther had earned two university degrees and was on course to become a fine lawyer. Then, in the summer of 1505, his life took an unexpected turn. He was caught in a severe thunderstorm while travelling between two towns. Lightning was striking all around him and he was terrified. At one point a bolt of lightening struck very close to him, narrowly missing him. Convinced that he was about to die, Luther threw himself to the ground and cried out to God to save him. He pledged that if God saved him from the storm, he would become a monk. He did survive and he was true to his word. He joined an Augustinian monastery in Erfurt on July 17, 1505, much to his family's disappointment.

Like most people of his time, Luther had a belief in God but absolutely no understanding of the gospel of grace. He threw himself into monastic life, trying to earn God's favour by his ascetic lifestyle and religious observance. However, no amount of self-denial and service could remove the burden of sin that he felt increasingly weighing him down. None of the sacraments and rituals of the Roman Catholic Church seemed to have any power to cleanse him of his sin and restore him to God. Fortunately, the head monk of the monastery, Johann von Staupitz, had a basic understanding of the gospel of grace, and led him in a prayer of repentance and faith in Christ, teaching Luther to cry out to Christ, "*I am yours, save me*".

In 1507, Luther was dispatched to Rome to carry some letters and accounts from the monastery to the Vatican. Luther had never been to Rome, and what he saw when he arrived there shocked him to the core. He saw priests visiting brothels, and churches charging poor people money to touch and pray to fake relics of supposed dead saints. Worst of all, he witnessed the outrageous selling of indulgences; priests selling certificates signed by the Pope, offering forgiveness of sins.

Luther returned to the monastery deeply disillusioned and angry with the institutional church. He was on the verge of losing his faith, when Staupitz, his superior, asked him if he had ever read the scriptures. Luther replied that he hadn't. Staupitz, sensing enormous potential in Luther, sent him to the University of Wittenberg to study theology. Over the next five years he was awarded two Bachelor degrees in theology and finally, in 1512, a Doctor of Theology. In October of that same year, he was appointed to the university faculty as "Doctor of the Bible". Within a few short years he became the most prominent and popular lecturer in theology in all of Europe.

As Luther continued lecturing, he became increasingly critical of the institutional church. His studies had revealed to him how far the church had strayed from the teachings of the New Testament. People travelled from all over Europe to attend his classes, and Luther's lectures became increasingly critical of the established church.

Matters came to a head in 1517, when Luther became incensed by the most recent sale of indulgence certificates for the forgiveness of sins, issued by the Pope in order to raise money for the building of a new cathedral in Rome. After witnessing many of the poor people of Wittenberg purchasing these certificates and believing that they were now forgiven of their sins, Luther decided to openly challenge the church. On October 17, 1517, he wrote a list of grievances he had with the unbiblical doctrines and practices of the church, listing them one by one. He sent this document, the 95 Theses, to his local bishop and also nailed a copy to the church door in Wittenberg for all to see. Coincidently, the printing press had only recently been invented in the nearby town of Gutenberg, and one of Luther's supporters took the copy of the 95 Theses from the door of the church in Wittenberg and carried it to Gutenberg for printing. Luther's 95 Theses became the first mass-printed document in the world. It was distributed throughout Europe and lit a fire that refused to be extinguished.

The publication of Luther's 95 Theses was just the start of his war on the established church. Over the next few years he continued to write books and publish papers, outlining the true teachings of the New Testament and pointing out the false doctrines and corrupt practices of the church. His ideas continued to develop as he researched and wrote, and by 1521 his writings had documented a long list of complaints regarding the false teachings of the church. These included:

- The Pope was not infallible
- Many of the previous supposedly infallible decrees by past Popes have contradicted each other
- The Pope and his cardinals, bishops and priests have no authority to forgive sins
- The Pope and his cardinals, bishops and priests are corrupt, caring more about money and power than people's souls
- Only Christ can forgive sins and he needs no priest or Pope to intervene on his behalf
- Jesus is our only priest, and people can enter into relationship directly with him
- Salvation is by grace alone, through faith in Christ, and not by any works of man or sacraments of the church
- The selling of indulgences (certificates of forgiveness) is corrupt and unbiblical
- The claim that relics (bones of dead saints) have magical powers to heal and work miracles is fraudulent and idolatrous

- Most of the supposed relics are fakes
- Charging money for people to touch the relics is corrupt
- The Bible should be translated into the common language so that ordinary people could read it
- The only valid sacraments are those mentioned in the New Testament – communion and baptism. All other sacraments are man-made and useless.
- Confession and priestly absolution, in particular, is a man-made sacrament that cannot bestow forgiveness
- The practice of issuing instructions for people to do penance in order to be forgiven perpetuates a false doctrine of salvation by works
- The bread and wine of communion do not literally change into Christ's body and blood – they are only symbols.
- Mary the mother of Jesus, did not remain a virgin after his birth

Initially, Luther was hopeful that the church could be reformed. He believed that if he could be granted a fair hearing in which he could point out the true teachings of the New Testament, that the church would see the error of its ways and repent. He was never given such a hearing. Instead, over a period of years and via several papal edicts and hearings, he was declared to be a heretic and was excommunicated from the church. The Pope ordered that all of Luther's writings should be burned and that anyone found trying to retain possession of them should be arrested. The Pope's soldiers travelled throughout Europe, going from town to town, burning Luther's writings in the streets and arresting anyone who resisted.

Luther, himself, was brought to trial in the town of Worms, on 17 April 1521 and commanded to repent of all his writings. He responded:

"Unless I am convinced by proofs from Scriptures or by plain and clear reasons and arguments, I can not and will not retract, for it is neither safe nor wise to do anything against conscience. Here I stand. I can do no other. God help me. Amen."

Luther managed to escape arrest immediately following his trial, and also narrowly escaped an assassination attempt which had been ordered by the Pope and his cardinals. One of the Princes of Germany, Prince Frederick of Saxony, hid Luther in his castle in Wartburg where he stayed for over a year, while the Pope's soldiers searched the country looking for him. During this enforced exile, Luther began translating the Bible into the common German language. When his translation of the New Testament was published in September 1522, the Pope declared that it was "blasphemous" for the Bible to be in the common language.

Luther's writings and his teaching lit a spark that became a blazing fire that swept around the world. His followers became known as Protestors or, later on, Protestants. Sadly, in the years that followed, many of Luthers followers were condemned as heretics and put to death by the church. Their initial desire to reform the church from within proved fruitless. After Luther's excommunication by the Pope, Luther and his ever-growing band of followers became a separate movement of Christianity. They discarded the sacraments and man-made rituals of the institutional church and began conducting their own church services, aimed at reinstating the practices and beliefs of the

New Testament. Their priests were allowed to marry and Luther published new liturgies and catechisms that guided the new movement in its affirmation of the teachings of the New Testament. The Protestant movement quickly spread from Germany throughout the entire world and sparked the Reformation - a period of great social upheaval and change where many of the established societal conventions were overturned.

There is much more to the story of Martin Luther, but this brief overview is sufficient to understand how Luther and the Protestant movement that he founded has had a lasting impact on the practice of Christianity today. Luther is regarded as hero by Protestants today, and rightly so. He was unbelievably brave. He dared to stand up to the monumental power and authority of the institutional church, which literally had the power of life and death over the entire world at that time. At great risk to his own life, he dared to stand up and say, "You're wrong!". His teaching and writing was instrumental in founding a movement which re-established the beliefs and practices of New Testament Christianity, and his lasting legacy is seen in the millions of people who now worship God in Protestant churches all over the world.

This is not to say that he was perfect – not by any means! He was strongly anti-Semitic, sometimes writing highly inflammatory denunciations of the Jews. His writings against the Pope also sometimes went beyond reasonable discourse and strayed into harsh ridicule and vitriolic denunciations. In his later years, Luther expressed regret at some of his more extreme expressions of outrage.

But God has a habit of using imperfect people to achieve his purposes. And there is no doubt that Luther was used by God.

At this point, however, we are primarily concerned with how Luther and his contemporaries shaped the preaching of the gospel right through to the present day. The primary shift that occurred was a dramatic reaffirmation of salvation by grace alone, to be received simply by faith. Luther and his contemporaries completely repudiated the gospel of works and superstitious religious practices that the Catholic church had preached for centuries. They denounced anything that even hinted at a man-made, works-based system of salvation. They denounced the practice of instructing people to do penance in order to be forgiven for their sins, stating that this was salvation by works. Similarly, they denounced indulgences (certificates of forgiveness) and the worship of relics, and stressed that priests have no ability to mediate between man and God. In their preaching they pointed to Christ alone as the means of salvation, and simply implored people to receive his grace and forgiveness by faith.

This, of course, has been the central mantra of the evangelical church ever since:

"For it is by grace you are saved, through faith, and this not from yourselves, it is a gift from God, not by works, so that no one can boast." (Ephesians 2:8-9)

But Luther had a blind spot. He was so committed to removing any hint of works-based salvation from the teaching of his new movement that he down-played the role of ongoing repentance and the necessity of a changed life. Although he often used the words "faith and repentance", he interpreted repentance to simply mean a change of mind – ceasing to trust in religious observance or good works or anything else other than Christ for your salvation. In other words, we are to repent of our man-made efforts to be forgiven, realising that we are too sinful to ever succeed, and trust in Christ and Christ alone.

While Luther's understanding of repentance was accurate to a point, it does not go far enough. It does not acknowledge Christ's insistence that those who follow him should exhibit a changed life:

"If you love me you will <u>obey my commands</u>" (John 14:15)

In fact, Luther went out of his way to avoid any hint that obedience and a subsequent changed life is an essential condition for ongoing salvation. This is most notably seen in his dislike of the book of James. The epistle of James in the New Testament is replete with strong exhortations about the necessity of faith to be accompanied by works – a changed life – if a person is to be saved. Again and again, James stressed the point that faith, if it is not accompanied by works of repentance, cannot save a person:

"Faith by itself, if it is not accompanied by action, is dead" (James 2:17)

"Faith without deeds is useless" (James 2:20)

"A person is considered righteous by what they do, and not by faith alone." (James 2:24)

"As the body without the spirit is dead, so faith without deeds is dead" (James 2:26)

Luther had great difficulty reconciling this continual message within the book of James with the message of salvation by grace through faith, found elsewhere in the New Testament. In fact, Luther had such difficulty reconciling James to the rest of the New Testament, that he questioned whether it was truly scripture, and was initially determined not to include it in his translation of the Bible. He described James as "a book of straw" and said that "it has nothing of the nature of the gospel about it", claiming that it taught salvation by works. In the end, Luther reluctantly included James in his translation, but placed it at the very back, as if to de-emphasise its importance.

Luther is not alone in his difficulty in reconciling the message of James with the rest of the New Testament. There are many today who struggle to accept its message. This is because Luther's overwhelming emphasis upon faith and his de-emphasis of works of repentance has flowed down to us through the centuries, colouring our understanding of the gospel. Those of us within the Protestant tradition are children of the Reformation, and our thinking has been profoundly influenced by the doctrines that were set in place from the beginning of the Protestant movement.

But the Bible does not contradict itself. This is an extremely important point to make. If, at any point, our understanding of different parts of the Bible leads us towards contradiction, it is our *understanding* that is flawed and not the Bible itself. Luther's conclusion that James contradicted the gospel of grace, indicates a flaw in Luther's understanding and not a contradiction within the Bible.

Unfortunately, among Luther's many wonderful legacies that

have been passed down through the subsequent centuries, this one deficiency in his understanding has been transmitted and replicated as well. Evangelical preaching today reflects such a preponderance of emphasis upon faith alone as a means of receiving salvation, that the need for repentance is completely overwhelmed. It is barely heard. In fact, most preachers are very wary of preaching too much about repentance, lest they are accused of promoting a doctrine of salvation by works.

It is the thesis of this book, however, that repentance is an essential component of salvation – both initial repentance and ongoing repentance. Luther completely missed the true meaning of the book of James, and many preachers today continue to do so. The mistake that Luther made, and that many people continue to make, is one of semantics. James is not attempting to ADD repentance or good deeds to faith; he is DEFINING faith. True faith, genuine saving faith, will always result in a subsequently changed life. Indeed, it must do so, or it is not faith; it is mere belief.

The book of James is not the only place in the New Testament where we find an emphasis upon the need for a transformed life. Jesus, himself, made this abundantly clear on many occasions. His clearest iteration of this truth is found in a parable with a truly shocking message. That is the topic of the next chapter.

3

A SHOCKING PARABLE

Arguably the most important passage in the whole Bible for our understanding of the gospel is a parable that Jesus told to his disciples, recorded for us in Matthew 18. It is such a crucial passage of scripture, that it is worth quoting here in full.

"Therefore, the kingdom of heaven is like a king who wanted to settle accounts with his servants. ^{24} As he began the settlement, a man who owed him ten thousand bags of gold was brought to him. ^{25} Since he was not able to pay, the master ordered that he and his wife and his children and all that he had be sold to repay the debt. ^{26} "At this the servant fell on his knees before him. 'Be patient with me,' he begged, 'and I will pay back everything.' ^{27} The servant's master took pity on him, cancelled the debt and let him go. ^{28} "But when that servant went out, he found one of his fellow servants who owed him a hundred silver coins. He grabbed him and began to choke him. 'Pay back what you owe me!' he demanded. ^{29} "His fellow servant fell to his knees and begged him, 'Be patient with me, and I will pay it

back.' *30* *"But he refused. Instead, he went off and had the man thrown into prison until he could pay the debt. *31* When the other servants saw what had happened, they were outraged and went and told their master everything that had happened. *32* "Then the master called the servant in. 'You wicked servant,' he said, 'I cancelled all that debt of yours because you begged me to. *33* Shouldn't you have had mercy on your fellow servant just as I had on you?' *34* In anger his master handed him over to the jailers to be tortured, until he should pay back all he owed. *35* "This is how my heavenly Father will treat each of you unless you forgive your brother or sister from your heart." (Matthew 18:23-35)*

This is a parable about grace. Grace that is undeserved and unmerited. Grace that is bestowed upon a hopelessly indebted servant by a merciful and benevolent King. Let us unpack the parable.

The first thing to note is that the servant's debt was huge: ten thousand bags of gold. Let's quantify this in today's dollars. At the time of this book's publication, the price of gold is nearly U.S. $2,000 per ounce. Assuming that a bag of gold would weigh approximately one pound, the monetary value of this servant's debt was roughly 320 million dollars. This man's debt was astronomical! That servant could work his entire life and never come close to repaying such a debt.

Jesus is quite deliberate in his depiction of such an impossibly huge debt. He is making a very important point here. That servant represents you and me. He represents every human being's position in regard to their standing before a holy God. Each of us, over our lifetime, accumulates such an astronomically large debt of sin that it is impossible for any of us to "pay it off". Our sins are so many and so huge that none of us will ever reach a point where we will have squared the ledger with God. No amount of good deeds can pay God back for the vast record of our rebellion against him.

There is a popular misconception in the general community that if I somehow manage to do more good things than bad things in my life, if my good deeds outweigh my bad deeds, it will be sufficient for me to be granted entry into heaven. This is a nonsense for three reasons.

Firstly, such a notion completely underestimates the vast volume of our sin, which accumulates rapidly every day of our lives. I examined this concept in detail in Chapter 1. The Bible tells us that we are far more sinful than we fully realise, with tens of thousands, and probably hundreds of thousands of sins accumulating over our lifetime. And even our good deeds are tainted with pride and selfishness and sinful motives. It would simply be impossible for anyone to accumulate enough purely good deeds to outweigh our sin.

Secondly, the whole concept of needing to "outweigh" our sin is also nonsense. It doesn't work like that. Even if it was somehow possible for someone to accumulate more perfectly good deeds than the vast volume of their sins, those good deeds cannot remove the sin from their life. The sin remains. Good deeds can't cancel out sin, like some kind of magic eraser. This is just common sense. Can you imagine a murderer or a rapist or a paedophile pleading in court that he be let off because he has only done the one bad thing and has done far more good in his life? The judge would simply say, *"Your good deeds are irrelevant. They do not cancel out your crime. You have committed a* *serious offence and you must face the consequences.*" The same is true with God. Good deeds cannot remove our sin. Sin is serious and must be punished, otherwise God is not just. A judge who, for instance, let a murderer go free because he had done more good things than bad would be sacked! Justice must be done, and criminals must face the consequences that are due to them for their actions. Our sins are serious and cannot be expunged by good deeds. Sin has a serious consequence, and that consequence is eternal separation from God:

"For the wages of sin is death" (Romans 6:23).

Thirdly, the Bible directly contradicts the misconception of a spiritual set of scales where God weighs our good deeds against our bad. The "spiritual scales" view of salvation suggests that the pass mark for entry into heaven is 51%. As long as you can tip the scales in favour of your good deeds, you've made it! But the Bible directly contradicts this view. Jesus said, *"Be perfect, as your heavenly father is perfect"* (Matthew 5:48). In other words, according to Jesus the pass mark for entry into heaven is not 51% or 60% or 80% or even 90%. It is 100%. Perfect obedience to all God's commands is what he requires in order for us to deserve entry into his perfect eternal kingdom. On this basis, just one sin is enough to bar us from heaven. Why? Because sin, at its heart, is rebellion against God, and that rebellion breaks our relationship with him:

"Your sins have cut you off from God" (Isaiah 59:2)

God's standard is perfection, and we have all completely fallen short of this:

"All have sinned and fall short of the glory of God" (Romans 3:23)

In fact, the Greek word for sin in the New Testament is ἁμαρτία (hamartia), which literally means to fall short of a target.

So, this is the first important application of the parable of the unforgiving servant: we have all accrued an impossibly large debt of sin which we cannot hope to "pay off". We cannot work our way out of this dilemma. We are completely unable to save ourselves. As important as this concept is, however, it should not be new to us by now. We have already examined this truth in some detail in Chapter 1.

The second important concept illustrated by the parable should be equally familiar: the extraordinarily generous nature of God's forgiveness. The King in this parable forgives the servant of his debt of ten thousand bags of gold. He completely wipes the debt. The servant is released with nothing further to pay. He is not put on a future payment plan. His future wages are not garnished. He does not have to do a zillion hours of community service to pay off his debt. He is simply released and his past debt is completely wiped clean. It is an incredibly generous gift that he is given. It is called grace, and it is given to him freely. It is unmerited. It is undeserved. It is unexpected.

In this sense, grace is free. But let us be clear about what we mean by this word, "free". Because, in the parable, it cost the King 320 million dollars to pardon the servant. It was free to the servant but not to the King: it cost him dearly. The King effectively paid ten thousand bags of gold himself to free the servant from his debt.

In God's case, it cost him even more to offer us a free pardon. It cost him the death of his Son. The grace that comes freely to us, comes at a great price to God. The grace of God is not the action of a benign deity who chooses to simply turn a blind eye to our sin. He cannot do that. A just and holy God cannot let sin go unpunished. No, in order for God to release us from our debt, someone else had to pay that debt. And the only person who could do so was someone who had not incurred a debt himself. It needed someone who was not in debtors prison along with us. Jesus, the eternal Son of God, the perfect one, was without sin and was the only one who could step in and pay for our sins. He was the perfect sacrifice, punished in our place, paying for our rebellion and suffering the wrath of a just and holy God so that we no longer have to. The King in the parable paid for his offer of grace with gold, whereas God paid for his offer of grace with the death of his perfect Son:

"For you know that it was not with perishable things such as silver or gold that you were redeemed ... but with the precious blood of Christ, a lamb without blemish or spot." (1 Peter 1:18-19)

In this sense, grace is free to us but incredibly costly to God. The fact that God was willing to sacrifice his Son, however, tells us of his extraordinary love for mankind. What Father would willingly sacrifice the life of his son or daughter for someone else? It is unthinkable. Yet this is precisely what God has done for us. Such is his love for us.

"For God so loved the world that he gave his one and only Son, that whoever believes in him shall not perish but have eternal life." (John 3:16)

Any questions of God's goodness are settled at the cross. Any doubts about his love are silenced by the unimaginably costly price he paid to save us. We may not have all the answers about why God allows certain things to happen in our world. We may not always clearly understand his reasons nor perceive the precise details of his plan in a specific situation, but his overwhelming love and goodness can never again be doubted. The cross of Christ is the ultimate, shockingly generous expression of his love toward his rebellious people. God loves you. Of this you can be sure.

Once again, this concept should not be new to us by now. To this point, this parable told by Jesus to his disciples has followed a familiar discourse – at least one that is familiar to most Christians within the modern church. We are saved by grace, and grace alone: grace which is free to us, but incredibly costly to God.

But the parable is about to take a surprising, even shocking, turn. It is a twist that we would not expect. It is a twist that is worthy of a modern day thriller. And it is a twist that directly contradicts two common Protestant beliefs: the concept of "once saved, always saved", and the de-emphasis of repentance.

Initially, the servant's debt is wiped away and he is set free. He is completely forgiven. So far, so good: this accords with the Protestant church's teaching about grace. But the servant then goes out and finds someone who owes him a couple of hundred dollars and demands payment. When the debtor asks for mercy and for more time to pay, the servant refuses and throws the debtor into prison. Upon hearing of this, the King orders the servant to be re-arrested. The servant is brought before the King again, and the King is furious. He says to the servant:

'You wicked servant! I cancelled all that debt of yours because you begged me to. 33 Shouldn't you have had mercy on your fellow servant just as I had on you?' 34 In anger his master handed him over

to the jailers to be tortured, until he should pay back all he owed. [35] *"This is how my heavenly Father will treat each of you unless you forgive your brother or sister from your heart." (Matthew 18:32-35)*

Do you see what has happened here? The servant's original forgiveness is *rescinded*. The grace that was originally given to him is now *withdrawn*. The debt that was originally cancelled is now *reinstated*. And the punishment that was originally waved is now fully enforced once more. At this point we must ask two very important questions. What has happened here? And, secondly, why did it happen?

WHAT HAS HAPPENED?

The servant who was once forgiven is now no longer forgiven. The servant who was once the recipient of the King's grace is now no longer in receipt of it. Or, to put it into Christian parlance, the sinner who was once saved is no longer saved.

I can already see your hackles rising. I can sense your upwelling of protestation. *"This can't be!"*, I hear you say. *"Once saved, always saved! You cannot lose your salvation! Once we turn to Christ in faith, we are saved forever!"* These are the mantras we have been taught from infancy within the modern Protestant church. The impression we are given from almost every pulpit is that once a person has bowed the knee and said the sinner's prayer, their ticket to heaven is signed, sealed and delivered, never to be rescinded. This doctrine is referred to as *"the eternal security of the believer"* or the *"perseverance of the saints"*. It proposes that it is impossible for a Christian to fall away and lose their salvation. This is based upon the belief that grace is completely unconditional: that once a person has been forgiven through Christ, their ongoing salvation is assured, regardless of the way they choose to live their life subsequently. Nothing they can do or fail to do, no matter how consistently disobedient their life may become, can cause them to lose their salvation.

But is this truly the message of the Bible? Is it what Christ actually taught?

This parable in Matthew 18 poses a serious problem for the *"once saved, always saved"* philosophy. I have heard people attempt to explain the parable away by claiming that the servant was never truly saved in the first place: that he was never a "true" Christian and, therefore, that his subsequent judgment and punishment do not represent a loss of salvation. But consider the precise words of the parable. Initially, the servant's debt is said to have been "cancelled" (verse 27). He was completely forgiven and set free. He literally walks away a free man, with nothing left to pay. His debt is cancelled and his punishment is completely rescinded. This is what it means to be a Christian, in receipt of God's grace. The King's declaration at the end of the parable reiterates this important truth:

"I cancelled all that debt of yours" (verse 32)

The parable leaves us in no doubt: the servant was originally completely forgiven; in receipt of the King's grace. He was saved! A clear and unfiltered reading of this parable leaves no other interpretation open. Any other interpretation can only come from bringing our presuppositions to the parable and twisting its meaning to fit with our pre-existing theology. Make no mistake about it: this parable teaches that a person can be saved and then subsequently lose that salvation. For that is the consequence that this unforgiving servant now faced:

"In anger his master handed him over to the jailers to be tortured, until he should pay back all he owed." (verse 34)

His original sentence is reinstated. He must now pay the full debt himself. And notice the severity of the punishment that he now faces. He is to be "*tortured*" and he is to be locked up "*until he should pay back all that he owed.*" This servant will never get out of prison! He will never pay back 320 million dollars! It is too big a debt to ever repay. Jesus intends us to be in no doubt as to what is being allegorised here. He is speaking of the agony and punishment of hell. He is describing the complete and utter loss of salvation that was once granted and is now rescinded.

This does not sit well with us, does it? All our Christian lives we have been offered the soothing salve of the eternal security of our salvation. In a subsequent chapter I will deal very specifically with the misleading doctrine of "once saved, always saved". But for now, let us consider the large body of scripture that describes either the conditional nature of one's ongoing salvation or the possible loss of salvation:

"Remain in me, and I will remain in you ... <u>If you do not remain in me</u>, you are like a branch that is thrown away and withers; such branches are picked up, thrown into the fire and burned." (John 15:6)

"<u>If you continue in my word, then are you my disciples indeed</u>" (John 8:31)

"Once you were alienated from God and were enemies in your minds because of your evil behaviour. But now he has reconciled you by Christ's physical body through death to present you holy in his sight,

without blemish and free from accusation <u>if you continue in your faith</u>" (Col 1:21-23)

"Hold on to your faith and a good conscience, which some have now rejected and <u>have shipwrecked their faith.</u>" (1 Timothy 1:19)

"See to it, brothers and sisters, that none of you has a sinful, unbelieving heart <u>leading you to turn away from the living God.</u> But encourage one another daily, as long as it is called "Today," so that none of you may be hardened by sin's deceitfulness. We have come to share in Christ, <u>if indeed we hold our original conviction firmly to the very end.</u>" (Hebrews 3:12-14)

"Therefore, my beloved, as you have always obeyed, not as in my presence only, but now much more in my absence, <u>work out your own salvation with fear and trembling.</u>" (Philippians 2:12)

"Therefore, my brothers and sisters, <u>make every effort to confirm your calling and election. For if you do these things, you will never stumble, and you will receive a rich welcome into the eternal kingdom of our Lord and Saviour Jesus Christ. (2 Peter 1:10-11)

"Now I would remind you, brothers, of the gospel I preached to you, which you received, in which you stand, and by which you are being saved, <u>if you hold fast to the word I preached to you</u>—unless you believed in vain." (1 Corinthians 15:1-2)

"Consider therefore the kindness and sternness of God: sternness to those who fell, but kindness to you, <u>provided that you continue in his kindness. Otherwise, you also will be cut off.</u>" (Romans 11:22)

"The one who endures to the end will be saved." (Matthew 24:13)

Can you see the conditional nature of salvation that is explicit

in these verses? You will be saved in the end, only if you persevere until the end. The scriptures are very clear that it is
possible to be saved and then to lose that salvation. It is
possible to receive God's grace and then fall away from it.

*"You are severed from Christ, you who would be justified by the law;
you have fallen away from grace." (Galatians 5:4)*

*"It is impossible for those who have once been enlightened, who have
tasted the heavenly gift, who have shared in the Holy Spirit, who
have tasted the goodness of the word of God and the powers of the
coming age and who have fallen away, to be brought back to repentance. To their loss they are crucifying the Son of God all over again
and subjecting him to public disgrace." (Hebrews 6:4-6)*

*"If they have escaped the corruption of the world by knowing our
Lord and Saviour Jesus Christ and are again entangled in it and are
overcome, they are worse off at the end than they were at the beginning." (2 Peter 2:20)*

Even the great Apostle Paul does not exempt himself from the
possibility of falling away if he does not remain vigilant:

*"But I discipline my body and keep it under control, lest after
preaching to others I myself should be disqualified." (1 Cor 9:27)*

This is the overwhelming testimony of scripture. It is, indeed,
possible to lose one's salvation. Hebrews 6:4-6 is particularly
clear. It describes people *"who have once been enlightened, who
have tasted the heavenly gift, who have shared in the Holy Spirit,
who have tasted the goodness of the word of God and the powers of
the coming age and who have fallen away"*. Make no mistake
about it: the people being described in this passage were definitely once genuine Christians and now are not. The interpre-

tive gymnastics required to claim that these people were not really Christians in the first place defies all accepted rules of hermeneutics (principles of biblical interpretation) and ignores the clear meaning of the passage.

How can this be? How can a person lose their salvation?

To answer this, we must return to the parable of the unforgiving servant, to answer the second important question: Why did it happen? Why did the servant have his forgiveness rescinded? That is the topic of the next chapter.

4

THE MISSING ELEMENT

I n the parable of the unforgiving servant in Matthew 18, what was it that prompted the merciful King to withdraw his mercy? What was the central issue that resulted in the rescinding of grace? What was the servant's key failure? Surely it can't have been a single instance of unforgiveness?

We must start by stating that this parable can't be inferring that in order to remain saved a person must never sin again. To go down this path would be to lead us back to the false doctrine of salvation by works – a doctrine that we refuted in Chapter 1. Just as one's initial reception of salvation is by grace alone, so is its ongoing retention. Salvation is by God's grace, from beginning to end. It is and always will be an undeserved gift. We never reach a point where we merit or deserve salvation because of our good living or perfect obedience to God. We live our Christian lives at the foot of the cross, needing Christ's forgiveness daily. Indeed, 1 John 1:8-10 explicitly describes this ongoing, daily need of the Christian to be forgiven for their failings:

"If we claim to be without sin, we deceive ourselves and the truth is not in us. If we confess our sins, he is faithful and just and will forgive us our sins and purify us from all unrighteousness. If we claim we have not sinned, we make him out to be a liar and his word is not in us." (1 John 1:8-10)

The verse immediately preceding this states:

"... the blood of Jesus, God's Son, <u>purifies</u> us from all sin" (1 John 1:7)

The verb, "<u>purifies</u>" (katharizo) in this verse is written in the present imperative tense, indicating that it is an ongoing process rather than a single event at one's conversion. In other words, we will remain in continual need of Christ's forgiveness every day of our lives. We will never be perfect.

So, given that perfection is not required in order to remain saved (otherwise no one would be saved!), what was it that caused the servant in the parable to have his forgiveness rescinded and his punishment reinstated?

The answer is that he was not transformed by the grace he received. He did not truly repent. He refused to extend that same grace to others and, by not doing so, he revealed that there was a critical element missing in his response to the King's grace. (Stay with me here! Because there is a very fine line between the teaching of this parable and the false doctrine of salvation by works.)

The King's grace was given to the servant freely and undeservedly. But it was not unconditional. Let me say that again.

Grace is free, but it is not unconditional. There is an important distinction. In the case of the parable, the King clearly required that the servant should begin to show others the same mercy that he had received. The King expected the servant to go forth and live a transformed life – a life transformed from the inside out by the undeserved grace he had been given. This expectation of the King is not explicitly iterated in the first half of the parable, but it is abundantly evident in the King's fury at the servant's lack of transformation in the latter half. Grace was given, but it came laden with an expectation; a condition. It was given freely and undeservedly, but its ongoing retention was *conditional* upon a major change in the life of the recipient; a response that was required.

The Bible has a word for the kind of response that God requires: repentance. The Greek word for repentance is metanoéō (μετανοέω), and it means a complete change of heart and mind, resulting in a changed life. It is a word that refers to an inner transformation which gives birth to an outer transformation. It is a determined decision to change the course of one's life, a decision which should be evident in manifestly altered behaviour and attitudes. Of course, repentance does not mean perfection. It does not mean that a person will never slip into sin again. But it does mean a firm resolve to turn away from past behaviours and attitudes, and to live under the new rulership of Christ. If repentance has truly taken place, the changes within an individual will usually not be subtle. They should be immediately evident. When God's grace comes to reside in a person's heart, when they have had a deep encounter with the forgiveness that is found in Christ, it will transform them from the inside out, by the power of God's Holy Spirit.

True repentance will be almost immediately obvious and evident in visible changes to a person's behaviour and attitudes.

The problem with the unforgiving servant in the parable was not an individual act of unforgiveness. That individual sin was merely indicative of a deeper, more fundamental problem: he had not been transformed by his encounter with the King's grace. His reception of that grace had left him relieved of his debt but unchanged in his heart. He arose and walked out of the King's presence essentially the same man as when he was arrested. He was unchanged. He was still greedy and conniving and unforgiving. There was no repentance. And his lack of repentance demonstrated his lack of appreciation for the gift he had received. He cheapened the gift, treating it off-handedly, as if it had no real consequence for his ongoing behaviour. He dishonoured the gift he had been given and, by so doing, dishonoured the King who gave it.

Let me reiterate a crucial point: grace is free but it is not unconditional. If grace was unconditional, then everyone would be saved. Let me say that again: **if grace was unconditional, then everyone on earth would be saved.** The fact that not everyone is saved, (in fact, the Bible indicates that only a relatively small percentage of mankind will be saved [Matthew 7:13-14]), tells us that there are *conditions* that must be met in order to receive God's grace. In fact, there are two conditions, and they are two sides of the one coin; faith and repentance. Grace is free, but it is not given to everyone. It is only given to those who respond to God in faith and repentance. Those are the two conditions. Grace is the gift; faith and repentance is how we receive it.

Furthermore, it is apparent from the scriptures that these dual conditions are not only required for one's initial reception of God's grace, but their perpetual operation is essential for the ongoing retention of that grace. Faith and repentance are not a single-use coin to be fully expended in initially purchasing our salvation – a salvation that we then somehow own outright and which cannot be taken from us. This kind of proprietorial attitude towards salvation – an attitude that says *"it's mine now, I own it and no one can take it from me"* - is what makes the "once saved, always saved" dogma so distasteful. A quick recital of the sinner's prayer falls far short of the scriptural conditions for salvation. The dual operation of faith and repentance is a ***lifestyle*** that God calls us to, rather than a single, momentary declaration. It is a lifestyle that the Bible urges us to persist in, day by day, year by year.

At the risk of undue repetition, let me remind you of several verses which clearly portray the essential link between persistent faith and repentance on the one hand, and salvation on the other:

"Remain in me, and I will remain in you ... If you do not remain in me, you are like a branch that is thrown away and withers; such branches are picked up, thrown into the fire and burned." (John 15:4-6)

"If you continue in my word, then are you my disciples indeed" (John 8:31)

"He has reconciled you by Christ's physical body through death to present you holy in his sight, without blemish and free from accusation if you continue in your faith" (Col 1:21-23)

"Hold on to your faith and a good conscience, which some have now rejected and <u>have shipwrecked their faith</u>." (1 Timothy 1:19)

"See to it, brothers and sisters, that none of you has a sinful, unbelieving heart <u>leading you to turn away from the living God</u>. ... We have come to share in Christ, <u>if indeed we hold our original conviction firmly to the very end</u>." (Hebrews 3:12-14)

"Therefore, my brothers and sisters, <u>make every effort to confirm your calling and election. For if you do these things</u>, you will never stumble, and you will receive a rich welcome into the eternal kingdom of our Lord and Saviour Jesus Christ. (2 Peter 1:10-11)

"Now I would remind you, brothers, of the gospel I preached to you, which you received, in which you stand, and by which you are being saved, <u>if you hold fast to the word I preached to you</u>—unless you believed in vain." (1 Corinthians 15:1-2)

"Consider therefore the kindness and sternness of God: sternness to those who fell, but kindness to you, <u>provided that you continue in his kindness. Otherwise, you also will be cut off</u>." (Romans 11:22)

"The one who endures to the end will be saved." (Matthew 24:13)

Faith and repentance need to be exercised continually, until the very end, if we are to be saved. Thus, in one sense, it is more appropriate to speak of salvation not as a completed event, but as an ongoing process – a process which remains dependent upon our cooperation with God via the perpetual operation of our faith and repentance. Notice how Paul, in 1 Corinthians 15:1-2, states that we "*<u>are being</u> saved*", thereby describing salvation as a continuously unfolding event, rather than something that is finalised and completed:

"Now I would remind you, brothers, of the gospel I preached to you, which you received, in which you stand, <u>and by which you are being saved, if you hold fast to the Word I preached to you</u>." (1 Corinthians 15:1-2)

Notice, too, in the above verse, that the unfolding nature of our salvation is contingent upon our ongoing necessity to "hold fast to the Word". In this verse we see both the promise (the free gift of salvation) and its ongoing condition (faith and repentance).

These twin conditions of faith and repentance are a "pigeon pair". They are inseparable. You cannot get by with just one and disregard the other. In particular, you cannot have true faith without repentance. The scriptures are replete with references to the essential nature of repentance for salvation:

"Repent, for the kingdom of heaven is at hand." (Matthew 3:2; 4:17)

"Then Jesus began to denounce the towns in which most of his miracles had been performed, because they did not repent." (Matthew 11:20)

"After John was put in prison, Jesus went into Galilee, proclaiming the good news of God. 'The kingdom of God is at hand. Repent and believe the good news!'" (Mark 1:14-15)

"Jesus answered ... 'Unless you repent, you too will perish!'" (Luke 13:3 and again in verse 5)

"I tell you that there will be more rejoicing in heaven over one sinner who repents than over ninety-nine righteous persons who do not need to repent." (Luke 15:7)

"Peter replied, 'Repent and be baptised, every one of you, in the name

of Jesus Christ for the forgiveness of your sins." (Acts 2:38)

"Repent and turn to God, so that your sins may be wiped out and times of refreshing may come from the Lord" (Acts 3:19)

"In the past, God overlooked such ignorance, but now he commands all people everywhere to repent." (Acts 17:30)

"I preached that they should repent and turn to God and demonstrate their repentance by their deeds." (Acts 26:20)

Since the Reformation, the modern church has placed a strong emphasis upon faith alone, as the essential condition for receiving God's grace. This, as was explained in Chapter 2, has been an understandable reaction to the appallingly ignorant doctrine of salvation by works that was perpetrated by the church of the Middle Ages. Martin Luther and other reformers rediscovered the wonderful doctrine of salvation as a free gift of God. They refuted the institutional church's works-based false gospel and proclaimed faith as our only means of receiving God's grace. But in their enthusiasm to overturn the false reliance upon good works and religious observance, Luther and the others played down the importance of repentance in the salvation process. In fact, repentance barely gets a mention in their preaching and writing, so strong was their desire to promote faith as the sole means of acquiring God's grace.

The lasting heritage of the Reformation is that the modern church has continued to emphasise salvation through faith alone, and rarely mentions repentance. When was the last time you heard more than a passing reference to repentance in a church sermon? How often do your preachers plead with people to turn from sin and repent of their disobedience to

God's commands? Repentance is the missing element in the modern church's version of the gospel, and as we shall see in the next chapter, its absence is having a serious impact on the kind of disciples that are being produced.

The Bible teaches that you cannot have true faith without repentance. If there is no genuine repentance, no changing of behaviour to henceforth live under the Lordship of Christ, it is just belief that a person is displaying and not true faith. This, in fact, is the key message of the whole book of James – a book which Martin Luther struggled to reconcile with the rest of the New Testament and which he almost excluded from his translation of the Bible (eventually and reluctantly including it, placing it at the very end of the New Testament). Luther regarded the book of James, as well as the New Testament's many pleas for people to repent, as being contrary to the message of salvation by grace through faith. Yet this is not the case at all. Repentance is the practical outworking of faith; the means by which faith is proved to be genuine. James, the writer of the biblical epistle named after him, understood this very well. Consider some of these statements:

"Faith by itself, if it is not accompanied by action, is dead" (James 2:17)

"Faith without deeds is useless" (James 2:20)

"A person is considered righteous by what they do, and not by faith alone." (James 2:24)

"As the body without the spirit is dead, so faith without deeds is dead" (James 2:26)

Reading through these and other verses in the book of James, it is easy to see how Luther and other reformers could regard these statements as contradicting the message of salvation by grace through faith, found elsewhere in the New Testament. On the surface, these verses in James almost seem to be promoting good works as a means of salvation, saying that faith is not enough. The mistake that Luther made, and that many people continue to make, is one of semantics. As I explained in Chapter 2, James is not attempting to ADD repentance or good deeds to faith; he is DEFINING faith. Faith, if it is genuine, will always result in a changed life. The inner transformation will give birth to outer transformation. It is inevitable. It is inescapable.

Just as fruit is the proof of the true nature of a tree, so repentance is the proof of the true nature of one's faith. An orange tree cannot produce bitter lemons. Similarly, a healthy tree will bring forth healthy fruit, but a diseased tree that has not been transformed on the inside will continue to produce diseased and withered fruit. Jesus himself used this analogy, at one point saying, "by their fruit, you will know them" (Matthew 7:16).

True faith, genuine saving faith, always manifests itself in a changed life. It is much more than mere belief – and this is precisely James' point:

"You believe there is one God? Good for you! Even the demons believe that!" (James 2:19)

In other words, just believing the right stuff does not save you. You don't have to convince demons that there is a God, or that Jesus is the Saviour of mankind and the Lord of the universe. They know this better than you and I do! But they are not saved, because they are not ACTING on that belief. It has not transformed them. It has not brought them to repentance. In fact, they are rebelling against it. Although they KNOW that Jesus is Lord, they are refusing to SUBMIT to him as Lord. Demons and Christians believe the same thing: the only difference is that the true Christian ACTS on that belief and demons do not.

It is the ACTION of repenting and submitting one's life to the Lordship of Christ that changes mere belief into saving FAITH. Jesus spoke about this often:

"If you love me, you will obey my commandments." (John 14:15)

"Anyone who loves me will obey my teaching." (John 14:23)

"Why do you call me 'Lord, Lord' but do not do what I say?" (Luke 6:46)

On one occasion, Jesus was scathing towards the Pharisees because of their failure to translate faith into obedient action:

"You brood of snakes! Produce fruit in keeping with repentance! ... Every tree that does not produce good fruit will be cut down and thrown into the fire!" (Matthew 3:7-10)

Jesus simply cannot conceive of the possibility of someone having faith in him without that faith resulting in a strong commitment to submit to him as Lord. Repentance is simply the practical outworking of true faith. It defines the difference between belief and FAITH.

The Apostle John came to understand the inextricable link between faith and repentance, writing:

"We know that we have come to know him if we keep his commands.

Whoever says, "I know him," but does not do what he commands is a liar, and the truth is not in that person." (1 John 2:3-4)

These are strong words. But we must take them to heart. We must believe them. A person cannot be saved without genuine, heart-felt repentance and a commitment to obey Christ as Lord. This does not infer that a true Christian will never sin. On the contrary, the Apostle John acknowledges that those who follow Christ will, from time to time, fall into sin and need to repent and seek forgiveness (1 John 1:9). The need for regular repentance is a simple acknowledgement of the reality of living with our fallen nature. Our obedience to Christ will never be perfect. Even more importantly, it will never bring us to a point where we deserve salvation. We will continue to fall far short of God's perfect standard. But repentance means that our hearts and lives our now heading in a new direction; one that will be inevitably and abundantly evident from our transformed behaviour and attitudes. It cannot be otherwise. If this is not the case, then we have not truly come to faith in Christ.

This was the essence of the unforgiving servant's problem. There was no repentance accompanying his belief in the King's goodness and greatness. There was no transformative faith. He remained completely unchanged by the grace he was given.

A final illustration might serve to illustrate the relationship between grace, faith and repentance. Imagine a swimmer caught in a rip at the beach. He is swept out of his depth and is being battered by large waves. He begins to tire and is in imminent danger of drowning. In desperation he raises his hand in the air, signally to the lifeguards that he needs rescuing. A lifeguard jumps into action, racing down the beach and plunging into the water, paddling out to the drowning man on a rescue board. Upon reaching the swimmer, the lifeguard holds out his hand and says, *"Take my hand, and I will lift you up onto my board."* The drowning man continues to struggle, however, thrashing in the water and trying to stay afloat. The lifeguard says, *"If you want to be rescued, you have to stop struggling and take my hand."* Eventually the drowning man gives in and takes the lifeguard's hand. He is hoisted onto the board and taken back to shore where he is deposited safely on the sand.

The drowning man was rescued by the lifeguard. He was not rescued by his own efforts. He was not rescued by holding out his hand. It was the strength and skill of the lifeguard that saved him, and the drowning man can take no pride in any aspect of the rescue. All he did was reach out and receive the salvation that was being offered to him. To do so, he had to believe in the lifeguard and trust that the lifeguard could, in fact, save him. There was a strong element of faith involved. He also had to stop struggling in his own strength. He had to cease his own striving.

Let us also suppose that the drowning man was holding onto something that was weighing him down – perhaps a large, heavy piece of coral that he had found before he was swept out of his depth. The lifeguard would have had to command him to drop it – to let it go – in order to be saved. This is a picture of repentance. We cannot be saved while still holding onto the sinful habits of our old life. Christ says to us, *"If you want me to save you, you must drop those things; you must leave them behind. I cannot take you on board while you still cling to those harmful habits and behaviours."* The drowning man then has a choice. *"Do I trust the rescuer enough to obey him and let go of these things, or will*

I refuse to let them go?" In this sense, repentance and faith go hand in hand.

Faith and repentance are how we reach out to receive God's grace. They do not save us; God's grace saves us. Faith and repentance are simply the means by which we **receive** God's grace. The drowning man, when later asked by his friends, *"How did you manage to escape the rip?"* would be foolish to declare, *"I was saved by dropping the coral and reaching out my hand."* No. He was saved by the lifeguard. It was grace that saved him, not his own paltry actions. Dropping the coral and reaching out his hand were simply how he received that grace, but it was not a means of earning it or deserving it. His salvation was by grace from beginning to end.

We cannot conclude a discussion of the biblical necessity of repentance without pausing for self-examination. Have you truly repented? Has your faith in Christ resulted in an obvious change in your behaviour and attitudes? Have you begun to live under Christ's Lordship, seeking to obey him now and turn from your past sinful patterns? Has your faith in Christ and your encounter with the message of God's grace actually transformed you?

Or are you essentially unchanged? Are you still mastered by your old sinful habits? Do you still cling to unhealthy patterns of behaviour? Have you refused to let go of them?

If you have not repented and made a fresh start, turning to obey Christ as your Lord, then whatever it is you think you have, it is not faith. It is mere belief. Like the demons, you are an unrepentant believer, not a Christian. And Jesus would say to you, as he said to unrepentant believers two millennia ago"

"Why do you call me 'Lord, Lord' and do not do the things I say?"
(Luke 6:46)

Let me get very specific:

- Are you addicted to pornography?
- Are you involved in adulterous or illicit sexual relationships?
- Are you having sex with your boyfriend or girlfriend?
- Are you a perpetual liar?
- Are you a perpetual gossip and slanderer?
- Do you regularly engage in dirty, smutty jokes?
- Are you a constantly bitter, unforgiving person?
- Are you constantly negative and critical, seeking to tear others down and build yourself up?
- Are you ruled by pride and selfishness?

These are not the marks of a repentant Christian. These are not the characteristics of someone who has come to know Christ and been transformed by his grace. You cannot truly claim to be a Christian, a follower of Christ, while clearly not following him! If your life continues to be characterised by these blatant and habitual kinds of sin, with no serious effort or desire to turn from them, then you have not repented. You are an unrepentant believer, but not a Christian. You do not have faith; you simply have belief. Because true faith is demonstrated by repentance.

Sadly, the institutional church is full of people in this category. Sunday pews are filled with hand waving, hymn singing believers who give every appearance of being born again Christians, yet their lives beyond the church doors indicate that they are not really following Christ at all. They are not obeying him. There are even ministers, pastors and priests in this category. They put on a good Sunday show. They are good at what they do. They can preach a good message, they can hold a crowd, they use all the right words. They are accomplished at presenting an impressive spiritual façade. But their conduct throughout the week is not infused with the grace of Christ. They treat their staff contemptibly. They are power hungry and manipulative. They may be harbouring secret adulterous affairs. They may be addicted to pornography. They may be paedophiles. They may treat their spouse terribly. They may rule over their congregations with pride and arrogance.

Yes, there are plenty of people in the church who claim to follow Christ but don't: people who claim to be Christians but whose lives throughout the week are lived in perpetual and flagrant disobedience to the commands of Christ.

Jesus, quoting from the prophet Isaiah, lamented this kind of hypocrisy when he said:

"These people honour me with their lips, but their hearts are far from me." (Matthew 15:8)

Is that you? If it is, then you need to do something about it! You need to fall on your knees and repent. You need to drop the coral that is weighing you down and reach out in faith *and repentance* to the Saviour. Stop merely calling him Lord and actually start *obeying* him!

You will still slip up and sin occasionally. Your obedience will never be perfect, hence your ongoing need for his grace. But there should be a dramatic change! People around you should be able to see the difference. The grace of God is meant to transform us, from the inside out.

Did you notice the last line in the prayer that I asked you to pray at the end of Chapter 1? It said:

"I open my heart to you and ask that you will come into my life, fill me with Your presence, and <u>*strengthen me to follow you all the days*</u> <u>*of my life.*</u>*"*

It's that "follow" bit that is missing in some believers' lives. Has it been missing in yours? If so, then make a decision, right now, to begin to follow Christ as your Lord. Make a fresh pledge to turn from your sins, to truly turn your back on them, to let them go, to leave them behind, and begin to truly follow and obey Christ Jesus as your Lord and Saviour.

If that is your heart's desire, then here is a prayer you might like to pray:

"Lord Jesus, I confess that I have followed you in word only. My lips have confessed your name, but my life has denied your Lordship. I have not followed you as I should. I have lived in disobedience to your commands. In particular, I have ....

Please forgive me. I kneel before you now, and pledge to follow you as my Lord. Please strengthen me to turn from sin and walk in newness of life. Please transform me from the inside out, by the power of your Holy Spirit, so that my life will glorify you from this day forward. I thank you for your grace, given so freely but at such a terrible cost to you. Thank you that through your death on the cross and your resurrection from the dead, I can be forgiven. Please help me to now live a life that honours you and reflects your grace to everyone around me. Amen."

5

A MODERN-DAY PLAGUE

I recently had a conversation with a youth minister who had been on the staff of a very large church. It is the biggest church in that part of the city, and if you are a teenager, it's the place to be on a Sunday night. Their Sunday evening service is pumping! The band is hot. The worship leaders are incredibly gifted singers and performers. The lighting is spectacular and the sound system is state-of-the-art.

And then there is the congregation. The large auditorium is literally jam-packed with teenagers and young adults. Hundreds of them! I've attended their evening service a few times, and it has an unmistakable energy to it. I found myself in the midst of a sea of singing, praising, jumping, dancing young people who are shouting out the name of Jesus, with hands raised and eyes closed in outward displays of heartfelt worship.

The sermon, each time I have attended, has been full of life-building, faith-inspiring stories interspersed with constant affirmations of our worth as unique individuals with gifts and abilities. The messages are full of promises of God's desire to bless us and help us reach our full potential. Every time I attended, the audience loved it. They lapped it up. The young people left the service feeling pumped up and inspired to be the earth-shaking, world-changing generation that God was calling them to be.

When I spoke with the youth minister, who has now left that church, I asked him what the greatest challenge was that was facing the young people in that church. Without a moment's hesitation, he responded, "Sexual immorality." Impressed with his candour, I pushed on and asked him what percentage of young people within the church were NOT sleeping with their boyfriend or girlfriend. He answered, *"Very few. Sex before marriage is the norm now among young Christians. Very few are remaining celibate until marriage."* I was shocked. But I was about to be shocked even more, because he then confessed that even among the single people on staff at the church (and there were about a dozen full-time and part-time staff) some of them tended to engage in sex when they were in a reasonably committed, long-term relationship. Now I was truly stunned!

Sadly, this is not an isolated case. Sexual promiscuity is a plague that is now endemic within youth groups and churches worldwide. The private, hidden nature of this disease is difficult to quantify, but there are some alarming statistics that are beginning to emerge from reputable sociological studies.

A 2009 American survey entitled the "National Survey of Reproductive and Contraceptive Knowledge", conducted by the Guttmacher Centre For Population Research Innovation and Dissemination, published the following figures:

- 42% of unmarried evangelical Christians, aged 18-29, were, at the time of the survey, currently in a sexual relationship outside of marriage.
- Only 20% of unmarried evangelical Christians, aged 18-29, have never had sex.

Admittedly, the study was limited, based upon a sample size of only 1,800 church-attending young adults. Plus, it is now considerably out of date. But the anonymous nature of the survey ensured a reasonable snapshot of the state of affairs within the Christian church at that time – a snapshot that has apparently not improved in the years since.

A peer-reviewed 2011 study of Christians within nine Southern Baptist Churches in the United States, by Janet E. Rosenbaum and Byron Weathersbee, entitled *"True Love Waits: Do Southern Baptists? Premarital Sexual Behaviour Among Newly Married Southern Baptist Sunday School Students"*, found the following:

- 70% of respondents reported having had sex before marriage while they were active church members.
- In six of the nine churches, the figure for premarital sex was 80%.

A more recent American survey, the General Social Survey, conducted from 2014 to 2018, found that only 37% of evangelical Christians believed that sex outside of marriage was *"always wrong"*, while 41% said it was *"not wrong at all"*.

The most recent and largest study of its kind is the National Survey of Family Growth (NSFG) that was conducted in America from 2013 to 2017, with its most recent findings released in December 2018. The study reveals the following statistics for active church members, aged 18-22, who have had sex outside of marriage:

- 65% of evangelical Protestants
- 74% of mainline (traditional) Protestants
- 80% of "black" Protestants (the survey's description, not mine)
- 72% of Catholics

Additionally, the study provides statistical data for active church members, aged 15-17, who have had sex outside of marriage:

- 26% of evangelical Protestants
- 26% of mainline (traditional) Protestants
- 35% of black Protestants
- 23% of Catholics

(I'm not sure why the study needed to differentiate "black" Protestants!)

There is no doubt that sex outside of marriage is a plague that has infected the Christian church. Of course, the church has never been completely free of this virus. There have always been active, church-attending "Christians" who have strayed into sexual promiscuity, but in the past, they were in the minority. They were the exception, not the rule. The staggering change that has come over the Christian church in recent decades is the virulent proliferation of this practice, to the point where, today, over three quarters of church attending Christians have had sex outside of marriage by the time they reach their early twenties. That's right: three quarters!

How has this happened? There are two things going on here: two factors that have contributed to the spread of this moral disease.

Firstly, society's post-modern rejection of absolutes and the rise of moral relativism has seeped into our churches. Moral and ethical relativism simply asserts, "*you decide your own values and ethics, and no one can tell you that you are wrong*". A whole generation of young people have been so indoctrinated with moral relativism that they have come to regard the Bible's ethical and moral imperatives as outdated and obsolete – a set of values that might have been appropriate in the ancient world but which are no longer relevant in our new, liberated society. Many young Christians no longer have a clear belief in the inerrant, authoritative nature of the Bible. Therefore, they do not necessarily regard sex outside of marriage as a sin. The new sexual ethic among young Christians now appears to be that pre-marital sex is morally acceptable as long as it is within a committed or loving relationship. In this regard, the new Christian morality is indistinguishable from the sexually liberated morality held by many within our wider society.

The recent highly public reversal of faith by author and preacher, Josh Harris, is a case in point. Josh was previously a leading advocate for abstinence and pre-marital sexual purity and the author of "I Kissed Dating Goodbye", which urged young people to abstain from all sexual contact, even kissing, prior to marriage. Tragically, Josh now repudiates his previously held Christian morals. He exemplifies the new evangelical sexual ethic, claiming that there is nothing wrong with sex prior to marriage. Even more tragically, Josh went on to then reject Christianity completely, divorcing his wife at the same time.

So, the first issue that has prompted the alarming rise in sexual promiscuity among Christians is an external one: the rise of moral relativism and the accompanying rejection of absolutes by our post-modern society. Many Christians have been seduced by this modern mantra.

The second factor is an internal one: the removal of repentance from the gospel. Even in churches which tend to still uphold the Bible's moral and ethical teachings, repentance is not clearly preached. In many churches, the Bible's denunciation of sexual promiscuity may occasionally be proclaimed, but the imperative for a person to turn from sin in order to follow Christ is not clearly explained. The essential nature of repentance as an inextricable component of the gospel is not clearly preached. If it *is* preached it is often preached very briefly and almost apologetically, as an aside, with the words "sin" and "repent" either completely missing or barely mentioned. Preachers will speak of making a new start, or living life God's way, or making Jesus King and instead of oneself – all of which express biblical truth to a certain degree, but are so vague and unspecific that they lack any real impact. We have removed the confronting element of the gospel and rendered it innocuous.

The vast majority of gospel preaching within the modern church, focuses on the grace and forgiveness that Jesus offers and rarely touches on Christ's many strong exhortations to "repent" and "obey". The result is that young Christians are left with the impression that the way they live does not really matter. Their overwhelming concept of the God they worship is of one who will shower them with love and forgiveness, and whose primary aim is to help them fulfil the awesome potential that he has created within them.

Repentance is the missing element in today's gospel preaching. And the result of this diluted preaching is diluted disciples. Christianity has become a religion of "easy-believism". The God whom people worship makes no demands upon them. He benignly invites them to chart their own course and determine their own moral code. He exists simply to fulfil their needs and bless them. His goal is to lavish them with love and forgiveness, and help them achieve their potential.

Whether intentionally or unintentionally, this is the view of God that our pulpits are presenting. It is the view of God that we have instilled within our congregations generally and among younger Christians in particular. By removing the imperative of repentance from the gospel, we have created a god in our own image. A sanitised god. A safe god. One who gives much and demands little.

But this is not the picture of God that the Bible presents. It is not even an accurate depiction of Jesus. In the life of Jesus we see both the mercy of a loving God and the judgment of a holy God who will not tolerate sin.

To the woman caught in adultery (John 8:1-11), Jesus offered grace, *"Neither do I condemn you"*, followed immediately by the conditional imperative, *"Go and leave your life of sin"* (v.11). Jesus does not conceive of the possibility of a person receiving his grace and then continuing to live a life of disobedience. For this reason, Jesus is scathing towards the Pharisees because of their failure to translate faith into repentance and obedience:

"You brood of snakes! Produce fruit in keeping with repentance! ... Every tree that does not produce good fruit will be cut down and thrown into the fire!" (Matthew 3:7-10)

Jesus enlarges upon this theme when he describes the Day of Judgment:

"Not everyone who says to me "Lord, Lord" will enter the kingdom of heaven, but only those who do the will of my Father in heaven. Many will say to me on that day, "Lord, Lord, did we not prophesy in your name and in your name cast out many demons and in your name perform many miracles?" Then I will tell them plainly, I never knew you. Away from me you evildoers!" (Matthew 7:21-23)

This is a confronting passage. Jesus is clearly describing people who have exercised some kind of faith in him, and who, in the words of Hebrews 6, *"have been enlightened, who have tasted the heavenly gift, who have shared in the Holy Spirit, who have tasted the goodness of the Word of God and the powers of the coming age [and yet] have fallen away"* (vv.4-6). According to Jesus' own words, the reason these believers will be eternally condemned is because the grace they received did not result in repentance and obedience: they did not *"do the will of my Father"* (Matthew 7:21). Instead, they were *"evildoers"* (v.23). It is not a lack of *faith* that will condemn them, but a lack of *repentance*.

It is my deep concern that the modern church has filled its pews with believers who have only heard half the gospel and who will face a rude shock when they stand in Christ's presence. Today's preachers and church leaders must ask themselves whether they have proclaimed the full counsel of God, or whether they have diluted the message to give it a broader appeal. I am reminded of Paul's declaration to the Ephesian elders, when he met briefly with them on his way to Rome and certain imprisonment. Reflecting on his previous three years of ministry among them, he declared:

"You know that I have not hesitated to preach anything that would be helpful to you but have taught you publicly and from house to house. I have declared to both Jews and Greeks that they must turn to God in repentance and have faith in our Lord Jesus. ... Therefore, I declare to you today that I am innocent of the blood of any of you. For I have not hesitated to proclaim to you the whole will of God."
Acts 20:20-27)

Today's preachers must examine themselves and ask whether they have not hesitated to proclaim the whole will of God. They must evaluate their teaching in the light of the full biblical gospel and ask themselves whether they are truly innocent of the blood of those to whom they preach. For what is at stake here is people's salvation. The modern pastor's primary goal is not to fill his pews but to populate heaven, and what may be effective for the former may be extremely detrimental for the latter. A diminished emphasis on repentance and a sole focus on God's grace and forgiveness may be appealing in the short term but it will inevitably produce shallow disciples who quickly fall away when the superficial promises of the positive gospel do not materialise.

In fact, this is exactly what appears to be happening in churches which specialise in this kind of gospel. There is a well-documented phenomena known as the 'revolving door syndrome'. Simply put, this refers to the short-lived church attendance pattern that is particularly prevalent among churches that do not preach repentance and the cost of commitment that Christ demands. A large number of people are initially attracted by the overwhelmingly positive message and begin attending church, but within a few years the majority of them have left the church and no longer profess any kind of Christian faith. Of course, every church will experience this to some degree. This is what Jesus predicted would happen. It is the parable of the sower, come to life: some people will respond initially and then fall away. But this happens to a far greater degree in churches that proclaim the repentance-free gospel. They have a much lower retention rate of converts.

For example, census data from the Australian Bureau of Statistics, as well as data from organisations such as the National Church Life Survey, indicate a very high turnover rate of church attendees within certain denominations that specialise in the kind of modified gospel that we have been discussing. This is not surprising. Without repentance, there is no depth to a person's commitment to Christ. It is a shallow commitment, based upon what I can get out of it. And when the promises from the pulpit don't come true in the real world – when, despite all the hype and showbiz on a Sunday, a person does not experience the victorious, fulfilled, amazing life they were promised – Christianity can be easily discarded. Such a person simply concludes that Christianity "doesn't work".

I have lost count of the number of times I have heard someone say, *"I tried Christianity, but it didn't work for me."* My response is always the same. I ask, *"What were you told to expect?"* When they respond with something along the lines of God giving them a victorious, fulfilled, empowered, miraculous, amazing life, I say to them something like, *"Well, no wonder it didn't work! Because that's not what Christianity is primarily about. You were told a lie. You were only told part of the story."* The great tragedy of the diluted, repentance-free gospel is not only that it fails to deliver what it promises, but also that it inoculates disappointed drop-outs from the true gospel. Those who have "tried it" and been disappointed are much harder to engage in gospel conversation, because they are convinced that they have tried the real thing and it has been found wanting.

Of course, the other great tragedy of the diluted, one-sided gospel is that those who persist in it to the end may well find themselves on the wrong side of Jesus' judgment. If a person's commitment to Christ lacks repentance - if they express a faith in him as the giver of life, the healer of their hurts, the source of their joy, the well-spring of their hope, their protector and victor who will lead them to a life of abundant blessing – if they celebrate and affirm those kinds of rosy truths all their life but never turn from their sins, blatantly continuing to disobey his commands (and even dispute whether those commands even apply anymore), then they may find themselves cast out from God's presence on the Day of Judgment.

The writer to the Hebrews expresses it graphically:

"If we deliberately keep on sinning after we have received the knowledge of the truth, no sacrifice for sins is left, but only a fearful expectation of judgment and of raging fire that will consume the enemies of God." (Hebrews 10:26)

Jesus spoke of this coming judgment in Matthew 25, using 3 parables; the ten virgins, the talents, and the sheep and the goats. Significantly, all three parables indicate that it will be our *actions* or lack of actions that will be judged, not our beliefs or "faith":

*"Truly I tell you, whatever you did not **do** for one of the least of these you did not **do** for me. Then they will go away to eternal punishment ..." (Matthew 25:45-46).*

Repentance, turning from sin to begin to obey the commands of Christ, is not an optional extra. It is not a peripheral issue for only super-spiritual Christians. It is integral to the gospel. Repentance is an essential component of our faith response to Christ. It is the thing that distinguishes true faith from mere belief. Without genuine repentance, a person simply cannot be saved, and they are fooling themselves to even call themselves a follower of Christ:

"We know that we have come to know him if we keep his commands. Whoever says, "I know him," but does not do what he commands is a liar, and the truth is not in that person." (1 John 2:3-4)

6

THAT FOUR LETTER WORD

The New Testament ascribes to Jesus a particular four-letter title: "Lord". It is the Greek word, "kurios" (κύριος). It is an interesting word. It was a term of great respect, acknowledging a person of great authority. On occasions, it could be used to simply mean, "sir". For example, when Jesus encountered the woman at the well in Samaria, recorded for us in John's Gospel, the woman addresses him as sir (kurios):

The woman said to him, "Sir (kurios), you have no bucket, and the well is deep. Where do you get that living water? (John 4:11).

Kurios was also the word for the master of a slave:

"Slaves, obey your earthly masters [kurios] in everything" (Colossians 3:22)

There are many occasions in the New Testament, however, where kurios was used to denote the name of God:

"But Paul chose Silas and left, commended by the brothers to the grace of the Lord [kurios]" (Acts 15:40).

It is this divine meaning that the New Testament attributes to Jesus. For example, in 1 Corinthians, Paul says:

"I want you to know that no one speaking by the Spirit of God can say 'Jesus be cursed', and no one can say 'Jesus is Lord [kurios]' except by the Holy Spirit." (1 Corinthians 12:3)

Paul is making an important point. As a God-fearing Jew and former Pharisee, Paul would never have considered using the word kurios in its divine sense for anyone other than as a reference to the divine name of God, YHWH (the Hebrew tetragrammaton - the four-letter name of God without vowels). To call anyone else 'Lord' [kurios] in its divine sense would have been blasphemy. Yet Paul now uses the term in that divine sense to refer to Jesus. And the point he is making here is that that kind of extraordinary declaration can only happen as a result of the illuminating work of the Holy Spirit. The Holy Spirit has opened Paul's eyes to see Jesus for who he really is, God the Son, the divine eternal Creator, come to Earth in human form.

It is this sense of the supreme authority and divinity of Christ that the word kurios denotes. The word is used over 700 times in the New Testament, and on most of the those occasions it is in reference to the absolute authority of Christ as the divine ruler of the universe:

"So that at the name of Jesus every knee should bow, in heaven and on earth and under the earth, and every tongue should confess that

Jesus Christ is Lord, to the glory of God the Father."(Philippians 2:10,11)

Jesus is the ultimate Lord. This world may have many lesser rulers and masters, but Jesus is the ultimate ruler and master of mankind. He is the Lord of all lesser lords. When the Apostle John was given a series of visions of the risen and glorified Christ after he had ascended back into heaven, at one point he writes this description:

"His eyes are like blazing fire, and on his head are many crowns. He has a name written on him that no one knows but he himself. He is dressed in a robe dipped in blood, and his name is the Word of God. The armies of heaven were following him, riding on white horses and dressed in fine linen, white and clean. Coming out of his mouth is a sharp sword with which to strike down the nations. "He will rule them with an iron sceptre." He treads the winepress of the fury of the wrath of God Almighty. On his robe and on his thigh he has this name written: King of kings and Lord [kurios] of lords [kurios]" (Revelation 19:12-16)

What an extraordinary description of Jesus! He is the Lord (kurios) above every other lord (kurios). He is the ultimate authority over all mankind, and the Bible says that the day will come when every knee will bow before him and declare him to be Lord, either in heartfelt worship or abject fear and terror:

"Therefore God exalted Him to the highest place and gave Him the name above all names, that at the name of Jesus every knee should bow, in heaven and on earth and under the earth, and every tongue confess that Jesus Christ is Lord [kurios], to the glory of God the Father." (Philippians 2:9-11)

It is this high and mighty image of the risen Christ that we are encouraged to envisage in all that we do throughout life, bearing in mind that it is to the Lord Jesus Christ that we are all ultimately accountable:

"Slaves, obey your earthly masters [kurios] in everything, not only while being watched and in order to please them, but wholeheartedly, fearing the Lord [kurios]" (Colossians 3:22).

"So we make it our goal to please him ... For we must all appear before the judgment seat of Christ, so that each of us may receive what is due us for the things done while in the body, whether good or bad." (2 Corinthians 5:9-10)

This is what it means when the New Testament refers to Jesus as Lord (kurios). He is the ultimate ruler and authority over all the Earth. He is the King of kings and the Lord of lords, and he is the one who will one day judge all mankind.

Let me ask you: how do you envisage Jesus? What is the picture of him that you hold in your mind's eye? Do imagine him as a long-haired, bearded rabbi, wearing the robes and sandals of a common first century Jew and benignly walking the dusty trails of ancient Galilee? This, of course, was how he chose to appear to mankind during his brief sojourn on Earth, but it is not an accurate representation of him in his eternal state. His temporary physical manifestation over 2,000 years ago was a deliberately toned-down affair. It was a convenient means of communicating with us at our level, and so Jesus literally took our form:

"He emptied himself and took upon himself the very nature of a

servant, being made in human likeness. And being found in appearance as a man, he humbled himself" (Philippians 2:7-8)

But this is not Jesus as he is in eternity. The Son of God, as he existed from before the creation of the world and as he now exists again, is a fearsome sight. Only a few people have glimpsed him as he truly is, in all his heavenly glory. Saul, who would later become Paul, saw the briefest glimpse of the ascended Jesus as he was travelling to Damascus to arrest and persecute more Christians. That brief glimpse of the ascended, glorified Christ blinded him and he fell to the ground in terror!

The ascended Christ also appeared to the Apostle John in a series of visions. Listen to John's description of the first instance when he saw Jesus in all his ascended glory:

Then I turned to see the voice that was speaking with me. And having turned, I saw seven golden lamp stands, and among the lamp stands was One like the Son of Man, dressed in a long robe, with a golden sash around his chest. The hair of his head was white like wool, as white as snow, and his eyes were like a blazing fire. His feet were like polished bronze refined in a furnace, and his voice was like the roar of many waters. He held in his right hand seven stars, and a sharp double-edged sword came from his mouth. His face was like the sun shining at its brightest. When I saw him, I fell at his feet like a dead man. But he placed his right hand on me and said, 'Do not be afraid. I am the First and the Last, the Living One. I was dead, and behold, now I am alive forever and ever! And I hold the keys of Death and of Hades'." (Revelation 1:12-18)

Feet like polished bronze? A voice like a roaring waterfall? A sword coming out of his mouth? Face shining like the brightest sun? This is no mild, bearded, sandal-footed Galilean. This is not a safe looking Jesus at all! This is a fearsome, even terrifying Jesus! This is what it means to look upon the ultimate ruler of the universe: the Lord and Master of mankind. Of course, even this appearance to John was merely a convenient apparition to give him something to focus upon. For God has no particular physical form. "*God is spirit*" (John 4:24). He is omnipresent in every molecule of the universe. He cannot be limited to a particular place and form. This image of Jesus that was presented to John was simply a convenient means of Jesus interacting with him.

Nonetheless, it was a terrifying image, wasn't it? In fact, it was so terrifying that John fainted. His testimony that "*I fell at his feet and became like a dead man*" was first century parlance for fainting. They didn't have a word for "faint" in the first century. This was how they commonly described fainting. The image of the ascended and glorified Lord Jesus that was presented to the Apostle John was so terrifying that he, a hardened fisherman, fell down in a dead faint. He lost consciousness in the presence of the overwhelming glory of Christ.

This is the image of Jesus we should bear in mind when we call him Lord. He is the ultimate ruler of the universe, before whom every knee will one day bow.

And it is this Lord Jesus who commands all people everywhere to repent. He commands all mankind to submit to his Lordship and live in obedience to him. The central message of the Bible is that "Jesus Christ is Lord", and this Lord Jesus demands our heartfelt allegiance and obedience.

"*In your heart, set apart Christ as Lord*" (1 Peter 3:15)

This is a very different concept of Jesus to the one that is presented by the repentance-free gospel. In many churches Jesus is portrayed as the one who exists to serve us – to meet our needs. But the Bible says that it is actually the other way around: we exist to serve him! He is the Lord and we are his servants, not the other way around! The modern "me-centred" gospel is a dangerous and deceptive distortion of the truth. By failing to teach the Lordship of Christ and our need to repent and submit to his rulership, Jesus is often portrayed as a convenient celestial vending machine to give us what we want and make our life better.

FACEBOOK FOLLOWERS

Many people "follow" Jesus like they would follow someone on Facebook. They like his profile. They subscribe to his page. They read his posts. They even put some of his suggestions into practice. But we don't have to agree with everything he says, do we? We don't have to obey his every teaching, surely? We can pick and choose, and still like him, can't we?

No, we can't. Either Jesus is Lord of all, or he is not Lord at all. Either he is your Lord and Master, or he is not. But he can't be half your Lord. He can't be ruler of half of your life, while you keep the other half for yourself, to live as you please. You can't follow Jesus, like you would follow someone on Facebook. It's all or nothing. Jesus demands complete obedience and nothing less.

"Why do you call me, 'Lord, Lord' and don't do the things that I say?" (Luke 6:46)

THE HITCH-HIKING JESUS

Back in the 1980s, when I was driving my first car, I used to occasionally pick up hitch-hikers. Hitch-hiking was more of an accepted "thing" back then. I used to enjoy meeting all sorts of interesting people and chatting to them.

A lot of people think that becoming a Christian and "inviting Jesus into your life" is like picking up a hitch-hiker. Let me explain.

Imagine you are driving your car along a highway and you come across Jesus standing by the side of the road, hitch-hiking. You pull your car over to the side of the road and stop beside him. You wind down your electric passenger window and lean across. You ask him, *"Would you like a lift?"* and he replies, *"You need to let me in."* You find this response slightly puzzling, but you let it slide. You ask, *"Where are you headed? Are you going my way?"*. Jesus replies, *"I am going my way, not yours, and you need to come with me."* Again, you find this puzzling, but you decide not to question him further. You lean across and open the passenger door, saying, *"OK. Hop in!"*.

But Jesus does a curious thing. Instead of getting into your car, he closes the passenger door and walks around the front of the car until he is standing at your driver's door. He opens your door, leans in and says, *"Move over. I'm doing the driving from now on."* Now you are perplexed. *"But it's my car!"* you complain. Jesus merely responds, *"Unless you let me do the driving, I will not enter your car. I am not here to be a passenger."*

At this point you have a decision to make. *Do I keep driving the car myself, or do I let Jesus take control?* Something about Jesus prompts you to submit. You slide across to the passenger side and Jesus sits behind the wheel. Immediately, he executes a u-turn and starts driving back the way you had come. You complain, *"Hey! That's not the way I was going!"* Jesus responds, *"I know. You were going the wrong way."*

This is what it means to respond to Jesus in faith and repentance. When we accept Jesus as Lord and Saviour, we hand the steering wheel of our life over to him. We place our life in his hands. He gets to do the driving now, not us. He gets to determine the direction of our life, not us. He gets to determine our morals and ethics, not us.

You see, you can't pick up Jesus like you would a hitch-hiker. He doesn't enter your life as a passive passenger. He either comes into your life as Lord of all or he doesn't come in at all. A lot of people have stopped their "car" by the side of the road and invited Jesus to come in, but they are still doing the driving. They have continued on down the road, travelling in the same direction that they were travelling in before, with themselves still in control. They are still deciding their own morality. They are still disobeying some of Christ's clear commands. They are in for a rude shock! Because Jesus is not in their car. They think he is – after all, they invited him in! But Jesus is still back on the side of the road. He did not get into their car, because they refused to relinquish the steering wheel to him. Jesus refuses to be a passive passenger.

If Jesus is not Lord of all, he is not your Lord at all! And sadly, there will be many people on the Day of Judgment who believe they are Christians, who have "asked Jesus into their heart", but who will be condemned by Christ because they did not submit to him as Lord.

"Not everyone who says to me, 'Lord, Lord,' will enter the kingdom of

heaven, but only the one who does the will of my Father who is in heaven. Many will say to me on that day, 'Lord, Lord, did we not prophesy in your name and in your name drive out demons and in your name perform many miracles?' Then I will tell them plainly, 'I never knew you. Away from me, you evildoers!'" (Matthew 7:21-23)

This is why the Lordship of Christ and his call for us to repent is crucial! It is a message that has been largely excised from today's gospel and, because of this, many people have been given false assurance of salvation. They think they are Christians, but they are not. We are saved by grace, but the grace of God flows only to those who have turned in faith *and repentance* to Christ as Lord. The modern, sanitised version of the gospel, without a strong call to repentance, may be more immediately palatable for our modern world, but it is producing half-hearted facebook followers of Christ who will ultimately face his displeasure and judgment. We may be filling our pews, but we are not populating heaven.

7

TRUE DISCIPLESHIP

If we are to truly understand the gospel as it was proclaimed by Christ and taught by his followers, we need to come to terms with the concept of discipleship. But what is a disciple? Before we can understand what a disciple IS, we need to understand what a disciple WAS in the first century. Because when the Bible uses the word "disciple", it is referring to a practice, in fact a whole institution, that was very familiar to first century Jews, but almost completely unknown to us in the 21st century.

When we read this word "disciple" in our Bibles, we are reading it from a point of extreme dislocation, in terms of both time and culture. Discipleship is something that has not been practised for over 2000 years – not in the way that it was in the first century. So, to help us understand what the Bible means when it uses this term "disciple", I'm going to take us back in time. We're going to jump into a time machine, and we're going to go back over 2,000 years to the time of Christ.

Are you ready? Let's fire up the Delorean. Because we're going back! And where we're going, we don't need roads!

In first century Jewish society, almost every boy attended synagogue school, known as Bet Sefer, from the age of 5 to 12. Only boys from extremely poor families didn't attend, as they had to start work in their father's business at the age of 5 to help support the family. But every other boy went to synagogue school, where they studied their sacred text, the Tanach, (our Old Testament), and in particular, the Torah, the first five books. By the age of 12 the most gifted students had memorised huge portions of the Torah, and the very best of them had memorised the *entire* Torah. And I mean memorised, word for word. We find this difficult to comprehend, but in the ancient world where written material was scarce and expensive and where many people could not read anyway, they relied on memorisation to pass on important stories and mythology. This is referred to as "oral tradition", and people in the ancient world were very good at it. In today's world, where we have unlimited access to the printed word and almost everyone can read, we have largely lost this ability, but in the ancient world people were very proficient at memorising impressive amounts of information. Children were trained from a very young age to memorise large portions of important folklore and mythology.

Upon graduation from Synagogue school at the age of twelve, the majority of boys were apprenticed to some kind of trade - carpentry, stone masonry, butchery, fishing, farming, etc. But the brightest of the students, were chosen to be a disciple of a rabbi - a religious teacher. And the very best of the best, were chosen by the greatest and most famous rabbis.

It was an incredible honour to become a disciple of a rabbi. Only about one or two percent of boys were ever chosen. A boy who was chosen to be a disciple, left home and lived with the rabbi for the next eight years. He followed the rabbi everywhere and hung on his every word. His task during those eight years was not to learn the scriptures, because he had already done that - he had already memorised them - but to learn the Rabbi's *interpretation* of the scriptures.

A first century rabbi demanded four things of a disciple:

1. ABSOLUTE COMMITMENT TO THE RABBI

The rabbi became more important to the young disciple than his own mother or father. To give you an example, the Jewish Talmud, the book of religious instructions that all good Jews followed, stated that:

"When one is searching for the lost property both of his father and of his teacher, his teacher's loss takes precedence over that of his father. If his father and his teacher are in captivity, he must first ransom his teacher, and only afterwards his father." (m. Bab. Metz. 2:11)

Thus, the disciple's commitment to his rabbi was greater than his commitment to his own family.

The second aspect of discipleship was ...

2. SACRIFICE

The life of a disciple required great sacrifice, particularly if you were discipled to a lesser known rabbi. Your life as a disciple would often involve very austere conditions, travelling the countryside, preaching in towns and villages, and living in the open without a roof over your head. Most rabbis were actually quite poor, living off the goodwill and hospitality of the villages and towns where they visited and preached. Being a disciple was often a life of sacrifice.

The third aspect of discipleship was ...

3. EMULATION

The primary goal of a disciple was to emulate his master: to learn to think and speak and act just as his master did. A disciple tried to emulate his master in every tiny detail - how he ate, how he walked, how he spoke. The disciple became a "mini me" of the rabbi. There was actually an incident in the first century when a disciple hid in the bedroom of his rabbi to see how the rabbi was intimate with his wife, so that he, the disciple, could emulate his rabbi when he eventually had a wife! (Please don't try this with the minister of your church!)

The fourth aspect of discipleship was ...

4. SUBMISSION

In the first century, a rabbi had complete authority over his disciple, and it was the disciple's responsibility to submit immediately, unquestioningly and perfectly to the rabbi's every instruction or demand. A disciple who did not obey his rabbi's commands would soon find himself back home with his parents.

This was the world of rabbis and disciples in the first century. There were hundreds of rabbis wandering all over the countryside of Israel, and they all had disciples. Lesser known rabbis only had a few disciples. The greatest rabbi at the time of Jesus had nearly 800 hundred disciples who had left their families to live in the rabbi's boarding school in Jerusalem.

DISCIPLESHIP UNDER JESUS

This brings us to Rebbe Yeshua Ha-Natzerim - Rabbi Jesus of Nazareth. When the Son of God, the creator of the universe, began his earthly ministry, he adopted this institution of discipleship for his own followers. And he insisted on exactly the same kind of devotion as did the other rabbis of his day:

In particular, he demanded the same four things from his own disciples:

1. ABSOLUTE COMMITMENT TO HIM ABOVE ALL ELSE

"If anyone comes to Me, and does not hate father, mother, wife and children, and brothers and sisters, yes even his own life, they cannot be My disciple" (Luke 14:26)

We need to understand that Jesus is using the word "hate" here, with a more relaxed Hebrew meaning, not our English meaning. In Hebrew the word "hate" could mean to simply love or value something less by comparison. It was a comparative term not an absolute. But Jesus' meaning here, however, is still very strong. A disciple must love him MUCH MORE than he loves anyone else.

Jesus had a constant stream of people coming to him and asking to be his disciple, but he made it really tough for them. He demanded absolute commitment. In Luke 9 we read of several responses of Jesus to people who wanted to be his disciple:

"Jesus said to another man, "Follow me." But he replied, "Lord, first let me go and bury my father." Jesus said to him, "Let the dead bury their own dead, but you come and proclaim the kingdom of God." Still another said, "I will follow you, Lord; but first let me go back and say goodbye to my family." Jesus replied, "No one who puts a hand to the plow and looks back is fit for service in the kingdom of God." (Luke 9:59-62)

These verses seem incredibly tough to us, don't they, reading them from the perspective of our comfortable lives in the 21st century? But this was completely in keeping with the practice of discipleship in the first century. Any rabbi was entirely within his rights to demand that kind of commitment. In fact the wider community *expected* the rabbi to demand this kind of commitment.

2. SACRIFICE

Like many rabbis, Jesus was an itinerant preacher, having no home and often sleeping rough. A disciple had to be prepared to live rough as well.

"Then a teacher of the law came to him and said, 'Teacher, I will follow you wherever you go.' Jesus replied, "Foxes have dens and birds have nests, but the Son of Man has no place to lay his head." (Matthew 8:19-20)

In the above statement, Jesus was referring to the itinerant, homeless lifestyle of his ministry. He was effectively saying, *"If you want to be my disciple, it's not going to be easy. You're going to have to endure some hardship. You'll have to give up the comforts of an ordinary life. It's going to cost you!"*

In Luke 18, a rich man came to Jesus and wanted to be his disciple. Jesus responded by saying *"Go and sell everything you have and give it away to the poor. Then come and follow me." (v.22).* But the rich man wasn't prepared to do that and he went away sad. Then Peter, having witnessed this exchange between Jesus and the rich man, said to Jesus, *"Lord, we have left everything to follow you." (v.28).* And Jesus replied: *"Yes, and no one who has left home or wife or brothers or sisters or parents or children for the sake of the kingdom of God, will fail to receive many times as much in this age, and in the age to come eternal life." (vv.29-30)*

The point is, the disciples of Jesus had left EVERYTHING to follow Jesus. This was not easy-believism; it was TOTAL COMMITMENT.

Jesus spelt out his insistence upon total commitment very clearly in Luke 14:33 where he said:

"So therefore, any one of you who does not give up all that he has cannot be My disciple." (Luke 14:33)

Similarly, just a few verses earlier, Jesus said:

"Whoever does not bear his cross and follow me cannot be my disciple." (Luke 14:27)

This is a metaphor of a dead man walking. It is a picture of someone who has put to death their own selfishness and their desire for comfort and security. It is a depiction of someone who is willing to nail all of that to the cross in order to follow Jesus alone. It's a really extreme picture of discipleship that Jesus is painting here, isn't it?

3. EMULATION

In Luke 6:40, Rabbi Jesus said, *"Every disciple, after he has been fully trained, will be like his teacher."* And in Matthew 10:24-25, Jesus says, *"The disciple is not above his teacher, nor a servant above his master. It is required for disciples to be like their teachers."*

In essence, Jesus said to the people of his day, *"If you want to be my disciple, you must become just like me. You must speak as I speak. You must act as I would act. You must live as I would live."* He called people to become a "mini-me" of himself.

4. SUBMISSION

The concept of submission was the foundational concept that a rabbi has complete and absolute authority over his disciples. It was what every rabbi in the first century insisted upon, and Jesus was no different.

In Luke 6:46, Jesus spoke to the crowd and said, *"Why do you call me Lord, Lord, but do not do what I say?"* In John 14:15, Jesus stated, *"If you love me you will obey my commandments."* Just a few verses later he repeats the same statement: *"Anyone who loves me will obey my teaching."* (John 14:23)

It is this concept of absolute submission to the authority of Jesus that is foundational to the concept of Christian discipleship. And these verses show that Jesus CANNOT CONCEIVE of a person being his disciple and NOT obeying him. It was INCONCEIVABLE to Jesus, just as it was inconceivable to all the other rabbis of his day

SIMILARITY

In all of this, in each of these four elements - commitment, sacrifice, emulation and submission - Jesus was no different from all the other Jewish rabbis in the first century. The high demands he placed upon those who would be his disciples, were no different to what all first century rabbis demanded. And as the number of Jesus' disciples grew from an initial 12 in the beginning, growing to at least 70 by Luke 10, Jesus continued to demand this kind of stringent allegiance.

BUT ... There were two key areas in which discipleship under Jesus was radically different from discipleship under any other rabbi. Jesus effectively blew apart the first century institution of discipleship by these two new radical elements that he introduced.

TWO RADICAL DIFFERENCES:

1. QUALIFICATIONS FOR DISCIPLESHIP

The other rabbis only selected the brightest and best graduates from the synagogue schools. But Jesus didn't give a rip about formal qualifications. He chose disciples based upon their heart. Because of this, many of his disciples were "unschooled":

"When they saw the courage of Peter and John and realised that they were unschooled, ordinary men, they were astonished, and they took note that these men had been with Jesus." (Acts 4:13)

This term "unschooled" means that these disciples had not been to synagogue school at all - some of them could not even read or write! This, of course, made Jesus and his disciples a standing joke among the other rabbis. One can imagine them saying, *"Have you heard about rabbi Jesus of Nazareth? Do you know whom he has chosen as his disciples? Unschooled fishermen who can't even read or write!"*

But this is an important illustration that the values of God's kingdom are not the values of this world. 1 Samuel 16:7 says, *"Man looks at the outward appearance, but the Lord looks at the heart."*

2. UNIVERSALITY OF DISCIPLESHIP

The second way in which discipleship under Jesus was radically different from discipleship under any other rabbi was in regard to universality. Jesus made discipleship UNIVERSALLY available – to anyone. For example, Jesus opened discipleship up to women. This was unheard of! It was outrageous! Jesus was a radical! There were a number of women who came to play a very prominent role in this own ministry and in the life of the early church, as key disciples. These included Mary, Martha, Priscilla, Euodia, Syntyche, Phoebe, Junia and many others.

As well as that, there was no upper limit to the number of people who could become his disciple. The rabbis of Jesus' day limited the opportunity to become disciples to only a select few – a limited number. But once again, Jesus turned this concept on its head. At the end of his ministry, as he was about to leave the earth, he gave this extraordinary commission to his disciples:

"Go and make disciples of <u>all nations</u>, baptising them in the name of the Father and of the Son and of the Holy Spirit, and teaching them to obey everything I have commanded you." (Matthew 28:19-20)

All nations are now invited to become his disciples! Jesus was announcing to his first century disciples that every person on earth is now invited to become his disciple. Not just a few dozen or a few hundred - millions and billions! He was throwing open the offer to every person on the planet!

So, there you have it! That was discipleship in the first century.

DISCIPLESHIP TODAY

OK. Now we need to jump back into the Delorean and come back to the 21st century. Now that we understand what discipleship meant in the first century, I think we have all the information we need to answer the question for ourselves: what is a disciple?

What Is A Disciple?

A disciple is a follower of Jesus. But not a follower as defined by our modern world of easy-believism. A disciple is not merely someone who attends church on a Sunday and believes the right stuff. No. A disciple is follower of Jesus, as defined by Jesus himself.

A disciple is someone who signs up to those four aspects of discipleship:

COMMITMENT: A disciple is someone who is totally committed to following Jesus above all else and above everyone else. To seek "first" the kingdom of God.

SACRIFICE: A disciple is someone who is willing to sacrifice their own comfort and desires in order to serve Jesus.

EMULATION: A disciple is someone who is absolutely committed to growing more like Jesus, their rabbi. To become like him in every way. To turn from sin and live a holy life, as he did.

SUBMISSION: A disciple is someone who is committed to obeying Jesus as the highest authority in their life. To submit to him completely.

This is what it means to call Jesus Lord. This level of commitment, and nothing less than this, is what Jesus demands of his true followers.

What Isn't A Disciple?

Let me also point out what a disciple ISN'T. A disciple isn't a super Christian: a level two Christian - as if there are the ordinary Christians on level one, and then there is level two Christianity, the super committed Christians, called disciples.

No. A disciple is the *only* kind of Christian there is. You are either a fully committed disciple or you are not. There is no such thing as a half-hearted, partially committed, lukewarm disciple. If you are half-hearted, partially committed and lukewarm, then, quite frankly, you are not a disciple of Jesus.

Jesus himself said this, in his warning to a bunch of half-hearted followers in the church of Laodicea:

"You are neither cold nor hot. I wish you were either one or the other! But, because you are lukewarm—neither hot nor cold—I am about to spew you out of my mouth." (Rev 3:15-16)

As I pointed out in the previous chapter, I think that some people believe that following Jesus is like following someone on Facebook. You like his page. You like what he says. You read his posts in the Bible. You even put some of them into practice. But you don't change your whole life. You don't do everything he says. You don't have to agree with everything he demands.

Oh, yes you do! Either he is your Lord, or he is not. But he can't be *half* your Lord. Either you are following him, or you're not. But you can't be *half* following him. Either you are his disciple, or you're just an interested onlooker.

So right here, right now, I'm asking you: if you had to place yourself in one of those two categories – true disciple or just a Facebook follower - which one are you?

You see, Jesus demands that we stop paddling in the shallows of easy believism, of part-time Facebook followership, and fully commit ourselves to serving and obeying him as a true disciple.

May God, through his indwelling Holy Spirit, strengthen you to live your life as a TRUE follower, a disciple of the Lord Jesus, so that, at the end, he will say to you, *"Well done good and faithful servant."*

If you have been a half-hearted Facebook follower of Jesus up until this point in your life, here is a helpful prayer you might like to pray:

"Lord Jesus, forgive me for being a half-hearted follower. I submit my life to you now. I repent of my selfishness and sin, of my laziness and complacency. Please help me to live for you now, and serve you with my whole heart for the rest of my life. AMEN"

8

THE ENCUMBENCY OF GRACE

At this point, I would like to introduce you to a new term: the *encumbency* (different to incumbency) of grace. What this means is that the grace of God, given freely and undeservedly to us, is also *encumbered* with the expectation of a changed life. Grace is given as a free gift by God, with the expectation that we will be subsequently transformed by it. God does not merely hope that this will be so, he commands it. We cannot receive his grace and then continue to live a life of sin and selfishness. Once we receive the grace of Christ, we must walk in a new direction, turning from our past sinful attitudes and patterns of behaviour and seeking to obey him. We cannot call Christ Lord, yet continue to wilfully disobey him. Christ's grace must result in a changed life, the evidence of which must be visible through our obedience to him.

Another way of describing this truth is to say that grace places a *moral imperative* on the recipient. Grace is given freely, at Christ's expense, yet it has subsequent moral obligations attached to it. It is not unconditional. God effectively says to us, *"If you accept this gift you are obligated to live a transformed life"*. Or, to use the biblical analogy of adoption, *"If you choose to become my child, you must live according to the family rules"*.

Those who accept God's grace yet refuse to submit to the "family rules" are effectively saying to God, *"I want to live in your house, I want to be forgiven and saved, but I don't want to accept your authority as my Father"*. Such people are only deceiving themselves and are in for a shock on the Day of Judgment.

"Be assured of this; no-one who is immoral or impure or covetous, or who worships idols, has an inheritance in the kingdom of Christ and God. Let no one deceive you with empty words, for because of these things the wrath of God will come upon all who are disobedient." (Ephesians 5:5-6)

This does not infer perfection among Christ's followers, for that will never happen. But it does infer a new resolve to obey and honour Christ as Lord.

Jesus clearly demonstrated this concept of the encumbency of grace: the ethical imperative that grace places upon a recipient. In a previous chapter, I referred to the woman who was caught in adultery and who was brought before Jesus for judgment. It is worth mentioning again, because it beautifully illustrates the encumbency of grace. To the woman caught in adultery (John 8:1-11) Jesus offered grace as a free gift, *"Neither do I condemn you"*, followed immediately by the conditional imperative, *"Go and leave your life of sin"* (v.11). Can you see that? Can you see that the grace Jesus gave that woman was *encumbered* with the expectation of a changed life? In fact, Jesus *demanded* that she live a changed life. His statement, *"Go and leave your life of sin"*, was phrased in the Greek verb tense that indicates an authoritative command. This was not a request or a suggestion. Jesus was not saying, *"It might be a good idea if you stopped committing adultery from now on."* It was a non-negotiable command. Jesus demanded repentance from the woman in response to his grace and forgiveness.

The clearest example in the New Testament of the incumbency of grace is found in the parable of the unforgiving servant that we examined in Chapter 3. It is worth quoting in full again:

"Therefore, the kingdom of heaven is like a king who wanted to settle accounts with his servants. As he began the settlement, a man who owed him ten thousand bags of gold was brought to him. Since he was not able to pay, the master ordered that he and his wife and his children and all that he had be sold to repay the debt. At this the servant fell on his knees before him. 'Be patient with me,' he begged, 'and I will pay back everything.' The servant's master took pity on him, cancelled the debt and let him go. But when that servant went out, he found one of his fellow servants who owed him a hundred silver coins. He grabbed him and began to choke him. 'Pay back what you owe me!' he demanded. His fellow servant fell to his knees and begged him, 'Be patient with me, and I will pay it back.' But he refused. Instead, he went off and had the man thrown into prison until he could pay the debt. When the other servants saw what had happened, they were outraged and went and told their master everything that had happened. Then the master called the servant in. 'You wicked servant,' he said, 'I canceled all that debt of yours because you begged me to. Shouldn't you have had mercy on your fellow servant just as I had on you?' In anger his master handed him over to the jailers to be tortured, until he should pay back all he owed. This is

how my heavenly Father will treat each of you unless you forgive your brother or sister from your heart." (Matthew 18:23-35)

This confronting parable is crucial for our understanding of the conditional nature of grace – the encumbency of grace. It provides us with the clearest insight of any New Testament passage into the relationship between grace and subsequent behaviour.

Initially, the servant has his debt wiped clean. *"The servant's master took pity on him, canceled the debt and let him go"* (v.27). Here is grace in action; freely given and undeserved. It is a description of the initial reception of God's grace at conversion; the complete forgiveness of sins, given as a gift, without any ability of our own to earn or deserve it.

The servant's subsequent unwillingness to forgive others, however, results in a shocking reversal of grace. *"'I cancelled all that debt of yours because you begged me to. Shouldn't you have had mercy on your fellow servant just as I had on you?' In anger his master handed him over to the jailers to be tortured"* (vv.32-34).

The grace that the servant had previously received from the master was taken away from him, because of his subsequent behaviour. Although grace was freely given, it was not unconditional. It came with a moral imperative affecting subsequent behaviour. It was **encumbered** with the non-negotiable expectation of a changed life. And because that moral imperative was not adhered to, the grace that had been freely given was cancelled. Salvation was lost.

In case we are in any doubt about this issue, Jesus concludes the parable with these sobering words:

"This is how my heavenly Father will treat each of you unless you forgive your brother or sister from your heart."(v.35)

The meaning of this parable is clear. This is one of several occasions when Jesus removes all vagary and speaks plainly. There is no subtlety here. The parable shouts at us: it slaps us in the face with its bluntness. The message is clear. Unless we are transformed by the forgiveness that Christ gives us, he will cease to forgive us. He will rescind his saving grace. He will remove our salvation.

This parable is extremely problematic for those who insist that grace is unconditional. In fact, the only way to cling to such a belief is to completely ignore this passage, for there is no other way of interpreting these clear statements by Jesus, without a violent rendering of the principles of biblical interpretation.

Let us be clear about this. Do we believe Jesus? Do we accept his words as authoritative and true? For that is the ultimate issue at stake here.

Why is a subsequent changed life so important? Why is it a condition of the retention of saving grace? Quite simply, because repentance and a changed life is the essence of true faith. Without repentance we cannot claim to be following Jesus as our Lord.

Failure to respond to God's grace with transformed attitudes and behaviour reflects a deeply inadequate appreciation for the depth of our own sinfulness and the magnitude of our own forgiveness. It reflects an appallingly shallow and off-hand attitude towards the depth of God's mercy for us. It cheapens his grace and fails to understand this important concept of the *encumbency* of grace.

In order to help us understand the incumbency of grace better, the next chapter will "put legs" on this concept by telling you a story.

9

A MODERN-DAY PARABLE

I would like to tell you a modern-day parable. You won't find this in the Bible. In fact, you won't find it anywhere else, because I made it up myself. Furthermore, I invite you to be the central character in this parable. Are you ready?

Imagine that you are a homeless person, living rough on the streets. Each night you scramble to find some kind of shelter to keep the rain off; sleeping under bridges, under shop awnings, on park benches or anywhere you can find that has some degree of safety and protection. You have no money and very few possessions. You live off the charity of other people, receiving barely enough each day for a hamburger and a cup of coffee. You are dirty and smelly, unkempt and bedraggled. You spend most days being asked to move on by police and shop-keepers: being harried from one doorway to the next. You have a few precious possessions that you wheel around in a broken down, rusty shopping trolley – a rank and filthy dog blanket to keep you warm at night, a flea-infested pillow that you scavenged from a rubbish pile, some cardboard to lie on, and a broken ukulele with only one string. You can't actually play the ukulele, but you sit on the sidewalk and strum it for hours each day and occasionally someone takes pity on you and drops a few coins at your feet.

On your regular rounds as you walk around the city, you pass by a beautiful mansion. Every day you stop and stare through the locked iron gates at the mansion, wondering what it would be like to live in such a place. The building itself is impressive: two stories tall, constructed of huge sandstone blocks, decorated with marble pillars and featuring a stunning set of marble stairs leading up to the grand double front doors. Surrounding the mansion is a stunning manicured garden, featuring a whole acre of magnificent trees and shrubs, paths and fountains.

A golden retriever usually roams the garden and, most days, it comes to the front gate to be patted by you. In fact, you have developed a special bond with the dog. You usually save a tiny piece of meat or hamburger bun to share with it, even though you are perpetually hungry yourself.

One day, as you are patting the dog through the cast-iron gates, a man in a suit walks down the driveway and speaks to you.

"Are you [insert your name here]?"

"Yes," you reply.

The man opens up the briefcase that he is carrying and pulls out a document. He explains that the owner of the house has recently died and has bequeathed his entire estate to you. He shows you the will, and you see your name clearly printed on it as the sole beneficiary. It is a stunning development! You have no idea how the deceased owner even knew your name. You thought you were completely invisible to society.

The man, who identifies himself as the previous owner's solicitor and the executor of the will, explains that there are two simple conditions. Firstly, you are not to bring your broken down trolly with its filthy contents into the house. You must leave them at the gate to be discarded via a council cleanup, along with the filthy clothes you are wearing. Secondly, you must maintain the property properly and abide by all the relevant council rules and regulations.

That's all!

The solicitor opens the gate and gets you to sign some documents. He asks you to remove your filthy clothing, which you do, somewhat self-consciously, leaving them with your other possessions. He then hands you the key to the front door, along with the keys to the Bentley and the Jaguar in the garage, and you walk naked into your inheritance.

The mansion is now yours. It is debt free. The previous owner had paid off whatever debt was owing on it. The estate is given to you as a free gift. You did not earn it. You did not deserve it. It is simply handed to you as an act of incredible generosity and grace. You rush inside and run through the mansion. You eat from the abundant provisions of the fridge and pantry until, for the first time in years, your hunger is satisfied. You take a shower and, also for the first time in years, you are clean and without any offensive odour. You shave and cut your hair. You put on clean clothes that have been provided for you. You are a new man (or woman).

This is a wonderful picture of grace: freely given and completely undeserved.

But there is more to the story.

Almost immediately, once you have taken possession of the property, you realise that there are certain conditions attached to it. There are council zonings which apply to it which specify what extensions may be done to it, how many floors it can be built up, and what sort of business may or may not be conducted from the home. You must now also pay annual rates. There are electricity bills and other utility bills to be paid. There are noise restrictions and rules that must be obeyed for the sake of your neighbours. You are also required to maintain the property so that it does not become a health concern or a public nuisance. If you allow rubbish to accumulate on your front lawn so that it becomes a significant problem to your community, the council can fine you and force you to clean it up. There are a myriad of local government laws and conditions to which you, as the new owner, are now subject, many of which have fines and penalties if they are broken.

A gift has been freely given, but it is *encumbered* with many ongoing responsibilities and conditions.

So it is with saving grace. When we become a Christian we receive something far more valuable than a house that will eventually crumble and rot. We receive a place in God's mansion, a place in his eternal kingdom, *"an inheritance that can never perish, spoil or fade"* (I Peter 1:4). It is given freely through God's grace, for it is far beyond our ability to purchase through any effort of our own.

Yet it is also ***encumbered*** with moral imperatives governing our subsequent behaviour: the need to walk in obedience to Jesus as Lord. It is ***encumbent*** grace. These two concepts, that grace is free yet also ***encumbered***, must coexist in our hearts and minds if we are to understand the true nature of salvation.

Our ongoing behaviour as Christians ***does*** matter. God insists on certain behaviour if we are to remain in his family. Salvation is not sealed simply by saying "the sinners prayer". This is why Paul exhorts us to *"work out your salvation with fear and trembling"* (Phil 2:12), and also why Jesus states that only *"those who remain firm to the end will be saved"* (Matt 24:13).

As the new owner of the mansion in this parable is now subject to the laws of local and state government, so the Christian who inherits salvation as a free gift is also subsequently subject to the commands of Christ. The grace that saves us is ***encumbent*** with the expectation of ongoing obedience to Christ as Lord.

"If you love me, you will obey my commands." (John 14:15)

"Whoever has my commands and keeps them is the one who loves me." (John 14:21)

"Anyone who loves me will obey my teaching. My Father will love them, and we will come to them and make our home with them. Anyone who does not love me will not obey my teaching." (John 14:23-24)

Christ promises the provision of a *"home"* (which he also calls a "mansion" in John 14:2) – but only to those who *"obey my teaching"* (verse 23). This is the repentance that he requires – a life that is transformed by the encumbent grace that has been given.

PART II

THE RISE OF THE POP GOSPEL

10

POP GOES THE GOSPEL

So far, I have discussed the loss of emphasis on repentance in Protestant preaching since the beginning of the Reformation in the 1500s. But in the last five decades, a new, disturbing development has been occurring. There has been a movement to sanitise the gospel even further. In an attempt to market itself to an increasingly self-focused world, the modern church has repackaged and rebranded the gospel message. The gospel has had a makeover and has emerged with a new cosmetically enhanced look. The blessings and temporal benefits of a relationship with God are touted loudly and enthusiastically to our consumerist society and those biblical elements that are seen as unduly negative or challenging have been subverted even further. The gospel is advertised as a great deal, providing people with a wide range of personal benefits. In this era of the shiny, new pop gospel anyone who persists in proclaiming the old biblical message about sin, judgment and the need for repentance is deeply frowned upon.

I distinctly remember my first sermon as the new Senior Minister of a church in Victoria, in 1995. On my first Sunday morning, I preached what I considered to be a safe message: a basic explanation of the gospel as explained by Paul in the first few chapters of Romans. I spoke about our created purpose to honour and serve God, our rebellion against God, the universal nature of sin and its dire consequences, God's rescue mission through Christ, His incredible sacrifice to pay for our sins, and the forgiveness that is now ours through Christ alone. When I returned home after the service, I received a phone call from the chairman of the elders. Without any pleasantries or preamble, he informed me that *"we haven't heard the words sin and judgment in our church for nearly 10 years, and we never want to hear them again!"* I responded by promising him that the church would continue to hear those words as long as I was their preacher, because I was determined to proclaim the complete gospel as it is declared in God's Word. To say that we had ongoing issues is an understatement.

What I experienced in that church is indicative of what is occurring throughout many branches of the modern church. The push is on to sell the gospel by highlighting and accentuating its wide range of attractive features and studiously avoiding any references to the ugly blemishes of its less saleable features.

Of course, the gospel *is* good news. But, as I have explained in previous chapters, we can only fully appreciate how good it really is by firstly understanding the bad news of our predicament without Christ. Mankind's rebellion against God, our resulting estrangement from Him, our slavery to sin, our looming judgement and, finally, the inevitability of eternal punishment, are all key elements of the gospel story. It is this bad news that makes the good news so wonderful! It is what makes grace so amazing! This is why the Apostle Paul devotes so much time to explaining the problem of sin and God's judgment in the first three chapters of Romans. The gospel is only good news if you understand our dire predicament. Furthermore, people can't or won't repent if they are unaware that they *need* to repent.

Dr Robert Schuller was one of the early pioneers of the refurbished, pop gospel in the 1970s. On one occasion, he made this comment, criticising the old gospel:

"What is that basic flaw [in the old Gospel]? I believe it is the failure to proclaim the gospel in a way that can satisfy every person's deepest need – one's spiritual hunger for glory. Rather than glorify God's highest creation - the human being - Christian liturgies, hymns, prayers, and scriptural interpretations have often insensitively and destructively offended the dignity of the person."

Schuller believed that preaching about such things as sin, judgment and hell were offensive to modern people. Instead, he crafted a new, sugar-coated pop gospel that proclaimed the power of positive thinking and promoted Christian faith as the means of achieving success and fulfilment in life. His rationale was simple: the gospel is a product, and, like all products, it needs to be marketed in a way that appeals to the perceived needs of common people. *"Find a need and meet it!"* was one of his catch-cries. And, as quoted above, Schuller believed that the major need that the church could tap into was people's *"spiritual hunger for glory"* (success, fulfilment, self-actualisation).

In an interview with Christianity Today, on August 10, 1984, Schuller commented:

"The church must develop a theology for mission. I don't think it's done that. I accept John 3:16 as a good one if people have a fear of hell. Maybe they have, but I find a lot of secular people haven't. At what point can I find a button to push so that I can reach them? I think their desire for self-esteem is that button."

Schuller's influence within the modern church cannot be underestimated. As his own church grew exponentially, countless thousands of preachers all over the world began to copy his style. The new pop gospel spread around the globe, finding its way into the pulpits of almost all Christian denominations.

The pop gospel is ubiquitous within Christianity today. Preachers from all denominations make the central focus of their messages about God wanting to restore broken people, heal past hurts, remove our shame, fulfil our potential, give us a life of purpose, help us achieve our dreams and do extraordinary things. Even conservative evangelical churches who decry many of Schuller's liberal excesses, have been subtly influenced by the pop gospel movement, evidenced by the rarity of sermons dealing with sin, judgment, hell and the need for repentance. The paucity of sermons dealing with these more challenging topics is completely disproportional to the proliferation of those same themes in the Bible, including within the teachings of Jesus himself. The Bible speaks a lot about sin and judgment; much more than most churches do.

The modern pop gospel embraces many concepts derived from pop psychology, particularly the concepts of self-esteem and intrinsic self-worth. Preachers will proclaim that you are a person of infinite worth with incredible potential, and that God's plan is to set you free from the insecurities, hurts, doubts, failures and fears that are holding you back, and enable you to become the person you were meant to be. Many preachers portray these things as God's central plan for your life. The fact that some of you reading this book may be wondering what is wrong with this type of message indicates how effective and pervasive this modern indoctrination has been.

Over the next few chapters I want to compare the true gospel of the Bible with the pop gospel of modern Christianity that has proliferated since the 1970s. In some instances, it may seem that the differences are insignificant, mere matters of nuance and semantics, but I hope to demonstrate how utterly destructive these embellishments are to the truth of the gospel and to its intrinsic power to save people from hell.

One of the foundational points of departure between the pop gospel and the true gospel of the Bible is the concept of a person's intrinsic worth. The pop gospel proclaims that you are a person of infinite worth with incredible potential, and that God's plan is to set you free from the insecurities, hurts, doubts, failures and fears that are holding you back, and enable you to become the person you were meant to be. This kind of message is endemic amongst Christian churches of all flavours. Preachers assure us that we are of great worth, that we are incredibly precious to God, and the proof of our inestimable value is the death of Christ for us. We must be incredibly valuable, otherwise Christ would not have died for us! I have heard this kind of message countless times from Sunday pulpits, from school chaplains and from youth leaders.

Dr Robert Schuller, one of the founding fathers of the pop gospel movement, expresses it simply:

"The death of Christ on the Cross is God's price tag on the human soul . . . it means we really are somebodies!"

This concept has a kind of superficial logic to it. Our experience in the world constantly reinforces the concept that the value of anything is determined by the price paid for it; the higher the price, the greater the value. Therefore, if the Son of God, himself, gave up his life for us, that must mean that we are incredibly valuable! We were worth dying for! An infinite price tag is an indication of infinite worth!

The problem with this pop gospel teaching is that it simply isn't true. In fact, it is a direct contradiction of the biblical gospel. The Bible teaches that we were NOT worth dying for, which is why Christ's sacrifice for us is so incredible! It is why grace is so amazing!

C.S. Lewis explains this succinctly:

"The infinite value of each human soul is not a Christian doctrine. God did not die for mankind because of some value He perceived in us. The value of each human soul considered simply by itself, out of relation to God, is zero. As St Paul writes, to have died for valuable men would have been not divine but merely heroic; but God died for sinners. He loved us not because we were loveable but because He is Love." (The Weight of Glory)

A wise friend of mine, Ken Collins, wrote recently:

"All one can conclude from the price paid for our redemption is the depth of God's love and grace. The more intrinsically undeserving we

are, the greater the measure of his love and the more mysterious His heart, and, far from making us feel good about ourselves, Calvary ought to make us feel good about God."

This is precisely the message of Romans 5:8 which tells us that *"God demonstrates his own love for us in this: While we were still sinners, Christ died for us."* In other words, Christ's sacrificial death does not indicate how amazingly valuable we are, it indicates how amazingly loving God is!

The church I belong used to hold an annual auction to raise funds for overseas missions. The strong philanthropic desire of church members to support missionary work was evident in the ridiculously large bids that were often made for the most mundane of items. On one occasion $1,000 was paid for a simple cake made from a packet mix from the supermarket! Was the cake worth $1,000? Of course not! The point is, a high purchase price doesn't always indicate a high value of the item purchased; sometimes it simply reflects the extreme generosity of the purchaser.

The disturbing tendency of the pop gospel to appeal to our vanity and prop up our self-esteem is in direct contradiction to the Bible. Jesus declared:

"So you also, when you have done everything you were commanded, should say, 'We are unworthy servants; we have only done our duty'." (Luke 17:10).

Similarly, Paul writes:

"Do nothing out of selfish ambition or vain conceit. Rather in humility value others above yourselves." (Philippians 2:3).

Elsewhere, Paul describes himself as a "wretched man" (Rom 7:24) and as the *"worst of sinners" (1 Timothy 1:16).*

If we are in any doubt concerning God's estimation of our intrinsic worth, we need only read God's summation of mankind in Genesis 6:5:

"The Lord saw how great the wickedness of the human race had become on the earth, and that every inclination of the thoughts of the human heart was only evil all the time." (Genesis 6:5)

The Bible's message is that we were NOT worth dying for: that we were undeserving sinners. This message is meant to bring us to our knees in repentance and lift our hearts in thanksgiving for God's fathomless love and amazing grace. The pop gospel, on the other hand, seeks to appeal to our vanity, and tickle our itching ears with assurances of how amazing we are. This is precisely what the Apostle Paul predicted would happen in the end times:

"Take note of this ... in the last days people will be lovers of themselves, lovers of money, boastful and proud." (2 Timothy 3:1-2)

The pop gospel's blatant appeal to this kind of vanity was also predicted by Paul in that same letter, when he wrote:

"The time will come when people will not put up with sound doctrine. Instead, to suit their own desires, they will gather around them a great number of teachers to say what their itching ears want to hear. They will turn their ears away from the truth and turn aside to myths" (2 Timothy 4:3-4).

It is very flattering to hear that I am awesome (a horribly misused word in modern parlance!) It is what my "itching ears" want to hear. It appeals to my pride and my vanity. But it is precisely this kind of over-inflated sense of self-worth that led to the fall of Satan and the rebellion of Adam and Eve in the beginning. When pop gospel preachers tell us how awesome we are, they are regurgitating the slippery-tongued lie of the serpent in the Garden of Eden. People who believe this lie will find it difficult to come to repentance, because true faith and repentance begins with acknowledging the depth of our depravity and our abject spiritual poverty.

We are not awesome. We are profound sinners, undeservedly loved and saved, not because of any intrinsic worth within ourselves, but because of the generosity of the God who is love.

11

WHAT ARE WE SAVED FROM?

I n the previous chapter, I described the pop gospel's slippery-tongued lie that we are all "awesome" (of great worth); a blatant appeal to our vanity in direct contradiction to the Bible's condemnation of us, in our natural state, as sinners. A second, equally disturbing lie follows on from this: a sugar-coated embellishment of the gospel that dilutes its power to save, and which has wormed its way into the pulpits of many churches today. It concerns the question, "What does Jesus save us from?"

The Bible's answer to this question is that we are saved from sin and judgment. Jesus removes the guilt of our sin by taking it upon himself, thereby saving us from condemnation, from the wrath of God's judgment and, ultimately, from consignment to eternal hell. The Bible paints a bleak picture of our true natures and our eternal prospects.

The purveyors of the pop gospel, however, have largely ditched the terminology of "sin", "guilt", "judgment", "wrath" and "hell". Apparently, these terms are not easily marketable to a modern audience. They don't sell well. Being told that you're an abject sinner heading for hell is a major turn-off to a generation who have been breastfed the lie that they are "awesome" and have unlimited potential. The bad news of the gospel is offensive; it offends our pride and vanity, because it tells us that we are a long way short of being as good as we think we are.

For example, Robert Schuller wrote:

"I don't think anything has been done in the name of Christ and under the banner of Christianity that has proven more destructive to human personality and hence counterproductive to the evangelistic enterprise than the unchristian, uncouth strategy of attempting to make people aware of their lost and sinful condition." [1]

Consequently, the pop gospel has developed a softer, less offensive set of concepts. Jesus is presented as the one who can heal my broken heart, remove my shame, restore my broken relationships and wipe away my past mistakes and failures. These concepts are drawn from the pop psychology movement of the '70s and '80s which championed self-esteem and self-actualisation, and they effectively make "me" the centre of the gospel. This kind of language pervades not only the pulpit in many churches, but also the lyrics of many worship songs. The effect of this diluted language is to significantly downplay the objective reality of my guilt as a sinner and portray me as a helpless, wounded victim in need of healing.

Let us examine some of this terminology to evaluate whether it is worthy of inclusion in the gospel.

"Mistakes and Failures"

Calling my rebellion against God's commandments mistakes and failures, instead of sin, diminishes both the seriousness of sin and our sense of personal culpability. "Mistakes" infers a sense of, *"oops-a-daisy, I didn't really mean that, it was an honest mistake"*, whereas much of our sin is blatant, wilful, defiant and downright evil. Similarly, "failures" infers that *"I tried my best, but I didn't quite do as well as I hoped"*, whereas sin, at its heart, is turning our backs on God and not even trying to please him at all. Let us be clear about this, we haven't just made a few careless mistakes and failures. We have sinned against Almighty God in thought, word and action, often knowingly, wilfully and deliberately. We (humanity) have lied, cheated, stolen, murdered, committed adultery, lusted, gossiped, slandered, envied, hated, held grudges, lived selfishly, not loved our neighbour, and not loved God with all our heart, mind soul and strength. To call this anything other than sin dilutes the gospel by diminishing our culpability.

"Shame"

Referring to Jesus as removing our shame is psychobabble nonsense. We need Jesus to remove our guilt, not our shame. Guilt refers to the objective verdict pronounced upon us by God because of the overwhelming weight of our sin. We have been found guilty in his courtroom and, unless we respond to Christ in faith and repentance, we are awaiting his just sentence. Shame, on the other hand, is an internal, subjective feeling that may or may not be accurate. I may be guilty and feel no shame, or I may be innocent and still feel ashamed. We don't need our shame removed. We need the cause of our shame to be dealt with – our objective guilt. If anything, people need to feel **more** shame for their sins so that they might more clearly perceive their guilt before God and turn in repentance and faith to the Saviour. Portraying Jesus as the one who merely removes our shame, presents him as the benign counsellor who helps us deal with our troubled emotions and feel better about ourselves. It is a particularly self-focused, superficial spin on the gospel – which is precisely what the pop gospel is.

The true gospel is much more profound: Jesus is the gracious Lord and Judge who offers death row criminals a free pardon. This, of course, is not a flattering picture of humanity, but it is precisely what we are. And what we desperately need, as we await execution, is not some smooth-tongued psychologist to visit us in our cell and help us deal with our shame, but someone to grant us a free pardon, open the cell door and set us free!

"Heals My Broken Heart"

Presenting Jesus as the one who heals my broken heart is another example of the self-focused superficiality of the pop gospel. I cannot find a single reference in the Bible promising that Jesus will heal my broken heart! There are several references promising that when a person becomes a Christian he or she *"is a new creation; the old has gone and the new has come"* (2 Corinthians 5:17). We are also promised that God will give us *"a new heart"* (Ezekiel 36:26). These kinds of statements, however, are describing dual aspects of our new spiritual reality – the change from being an enemy of God to now being reconciled with him, and the change from being led by our sinful nature to now being led by God's Spirit.

Neither of these new realities, however, involve having our past hurts miraculously resolved and healed. Instead, the scriptures command us to heal ourselves of past hurts by forgiving those who hurt us. Paul also speaks of *"forgetting what is behind and straining toward what is ahead, I press on toward the goal..." (Philippians 3:13),* indicating God's desire that we focus on our present and ongoing service for him, rather than introspective wallowing in the past. Furthermore, the picture of having my poor broken heart healed portrays me as the innocent, helpless victim who has been unfairly treated by this horrible world. This kind of imagery ignores any sense of personal culpability for the mess of my life and further perpetuates the self-focused, superficial, emotive wallowing that is central to the pop gospel.

Healing of Broken Relationships

Similarly, there is no promise in the Bible that Jesus will miraculously heal my broken relationships. Instead, we are given very clear and practical commands concerning how to forgive others and live in love towards them. It is *our* job to restore and maintain positive relationships with others, not God's; we cannot passively abdicate this responsibility. This is not to deny the fact that prayer, and God's intervention, is sometimes required to smooth the troubled waters of a damaged friendship, along with the wisdom and guidance of His Spirit to know the best way to proceed. To suggest, however, that a primary purpose of Jesus' sacrificial death on the cross was to restore broken human relationships completely ignores the life-and-death crisis mankind faced and makes a mockery of the cross.

What took Jesus to Calvary was not the need to have our shame removed or our broken hearts mended or our relationships restored. If that was all that was needed, Jesus didn't really need to die on the cross! We could have simply booked an appointment with a counsellor.

No, it was something far more serious that took Jesus to the cross. It was our evil, our sin; the weight of our crushing guilt and its eternal consequences. That is why God took such drastic action as to sacrifice his Son for us; to punish him in our place so that we could have our guilt wiped away.

The pop gospel is an insult to the cross. In attempting to market the gospel in more appealing language it has watered down its message into a kind of vacuous, self-absorbed introspection and rendered Christ as the benign counsellor of our hearts. In seeking to make the gospel inoffensive, the purveyors of this modern message have managed to render it impotent. For, unless people are taught the true depth and seriousness of their disease, they will never understand or appreciate the incredible nature of its cure.

12

WHAT ARE WE REALLY SAVED FROM?

In the previous chapter, I described the pop gospel's appallingly superficial response to the question, *"What does Jesus save us from?"*. It is a response rooted in pop psychology and crafted to dress the gospel in language that appeals to a self-focused generation. The true gospel, however, as proclaimed in the Bible, portrays Jesus as dealing with a deadly problem, the solution to which required the most drastic of actions. The pop gospel's appalling distortion of the truth is best demonstrated by comparing it to the true biblical gospel.

Although the problem of our sin has been discussed in an earlier chapter, it is worth exploring our problem in slightly more detail here. The biblical gospel starts with profoundly bad news:

We are sinners. *"All have sinned and fallen short of the glory of God" (Romans 3:23).* All of us break God's commands regularly. We covet, lust, envy, gossip, lie, cheat, steal, murder, hate, slander, hold grudges, dishonour our parents and swear. We are greedy, proud and selfish. We regularly fail to do the good we know we should. We do not love our neighbour as we should. And, worst of all, we do not love the Lord our God with all our heart, mind, soul and strength. There would be very few people who would not break at least one of the 10 commandments almost every day of their lives!

We are profound sinners. According to the Bible, we aren't merely good people who slip up occasionally. We are inherently evil. Even our best actions and efforts are tainted with sin. Pride, greed, envy, lust and selfishness underscore even our most noble actions. *"All of us have become like one who is unclean, and all our righteous acts are like filthy rags" (Isaiah 64:6).* The Bible's condemnation of our true natures could not be expressed more clearly than in Genesis 6:5; *"The Lord saw how great the wickedness of the human race had become on the earth, and that every inclination of the thoughts of the human heart was only evil all the time".* This is why even the great Apostle Paul described himself as a *"wretched man" (Romans 7:24)* and as the *"worst of sinners" (1 Timothy 1:16).*

We are hopeless sinners. The news gets worse: We are completely powerless to change our inner natures. Our evil is so deeply embedded within us that no amount of effort or New Year's resolutions can bring about true reform. The Bible describes us as *"slaves to sin" (Romans 6:20),* hopelessly chained to our sinful natures. In fact, this is our predicament from birth: *"Surely, I was sinful at birth, sinful from the time my mother conceived me" (Psalm 51:5).* Just as a lawn bowl is incapable of rolling straight because of its inbuilt bias, our own inbuilt bias makes it impossible for us to break free from our sinful nature and live a life pleasing to God.

We are condemned sinners. We stand already condemned before God, guilty of gross disobedience and only awaiting the final proclamation of our sentence: spiritual death – eternal separation from God in hell. *"The wages of sin is death" (Romans 6:23).* The final judgment will see us face the wrath of God for our disobedience: *"You are storing up wrath against yourselves for the day of God's wrath, when his righteous judgment will be revealed" (Romans 2:5).* Any person who optimistically believes that their "good" life warrants some kind of ticket tape parade as they enter the pearly gates has completely failed to comprehend the extent and seriousness of their sin: *"There is no one who is righteous; not even one" (Romans 3:10).*

This is a truly bleak picture. The gospel starts with the worst possible news: we are profound sinners, unable to reform ourselves, already condemned and awaiting the final execution of our eternal sentence. This is what Jesus saves us from! Not from shame or a broken heart or unfulfilled dreams or unrealised potential, as the pop gospel would have us believe. Only once we have grasped the enormity of our problem can we fully appreciate the extraordinary nature of the salvation that Jesus offers. Jesus, the sinless one, took our sin upon himself, suffering God's wrath in our place, so that we, the guilty ones, could go free.

"We all, like sheep, have gone astray, each of us has turned to his own way; and the Lord laid on him [Jesus] the iniquity of us all" (Isaiah 53:6).

Not only that, but, for those who turn to Christ in faith and repentance, he indwells us with his Holy Spirit, and sets us free from the enslaving power of our sinful natures.

"So, if the Son sets you free, you shall be free indeed!" (John 8:36).

This is the biblical gospel. It is incredibly bad news followed by amazingly good news! C.J. Mahaney, author of "The Cross Centred Life: Keeping The Gospel The Main Thing", declares:

"Only those who are truly aware of their sin can truly cherish grace."

The reluctance of many modern preachers to talk about sin, judgment and hell, is an inexcusable dilution of the gospel of grace. The pop gospel's self-focused message of Jesus as the fulfiller of dreams, healer of broken hearts, remover of shame and the one who can provide us with a fresh start in order to reach our full potential, is grossly negligent. It is akin to a doctor who fails to advise his patient that he has cancer and, instead, treats him for a cold.

Like every good lie, the pop gospel's message contains just enough truth to make it convincing and appealing. For example, Jesus does give us a fresh start – but not a fresh start to reach our awesome potential! The new beginning he provides is a restored relationship with God – transforming us from condemned enemies to friends and dearly loved adopted children!

By understating the deadly nature of our condition and, instead, pandering to our self-focused natures, the pop gospel's "inoffensive" message dilutes the true gospel of its power and, at best, produces shallow, self-centred Christians. At worst, its slippery-tongued message completely obfuscates the message of salvation, providing false comfort and assurance for unrepentant pew sitters.

13

HOW ARE WE SAVED?

I n previous chapters, we have seen that the post-modern pop gospel differs from the biblical gospel in the way it offers alternate answers to the questions, *"What is our intrinsic worth?"* and *"What are we saved from?"* A third question that provokes a divergent answer is, *"How are we saved?"*

Initially, the pop gospel seems to align with the teaching of the Bible in answering this question; we are saved by God's grace (Ephesians 2:8-9), made possible by the atoning death and resurrection of Jesus (1 Peter 3:18). A major divergence, however, occurs in the pop gospel's answer to a secondary question, *"What must we do to receive this grace?"*

The Bible's answer to this secondary question is clear; faith and repentance are the means by which we receive the free gift of God's grace. Please forgive me if I am repeating here what we have already dealt with earlier in the book, but it may be some time since you read those chapters and this is such a vital point it that it bears briefly repeating. (If you really don't need any further convincing about the true gospel's emphasis on repentance, just jump ahead a couple of pages to the next sub-heading, The Pop Gospel Message).

The dual elements of faith and repentance are inseparable and indisputable in the teaching of the Bible. In fact, faith without repentance appears to have been unthinkable to the biblical writers, constituting mere belief rather than true faith. The essential nature of repentance, in particular, is evident throughout the New Testament. Peter, for example, when asked by the deeply convicted crowd on the Day of Pentecost, *"What must we do to be saved?"*, responded:

"Repent and be baptised, every one of you, in the name of Jesus Christ for the forgiveness of your sins" (Acts 2:37-38).

This single passage perfectly illustrates two crucial concepts regarding repentance; its essential role in the salvation process (*"must"*), and its precise nature - turning from sin (*"for the forgiveness of your sins"*).

The Apostle Paul also points out the essential nature of repentance for salvation:

"Godly sorrow brings about repentance which leads to salvation" (2 Corinthians 7:10)

This absolute necessity to turn from our sins in order to be saved is evident in the teachings of Jesus:

"From that time on, Jesus began to preach, 'Repent, for the kingdom of God is at hand'." (Matthew 4:17)

"Produce fruit in keeping with repentance" (Matthew 3:8)

"I have not come to call the righteous, but sinners to repentance"
(Luke 5:31-32)

"The Messiah will suffer and rise from the dead on the third day, and
repentance for the forgiveness of sins will be preached in his name to
all nations" (Luke 24:46-47)

Significantly, this last statement by Jesus indicates both the
means by which grace is made available (his death and resurrection) and the means by which we procure it (repentance).

Furthermore, the New Testament provides us with a picture of
the robust nature of the repentance that must accompany true
saving faith. It involves more than the mere recitation of a
simple prayer. True repentance is a radical realignment of one's
life to bring it under the Lordship of Christ. It means changing
the way we live in order to begin to live in obedience to the
teachings and commandments of Christ. This will always
involve making profound and practical changes to stop sinning
and start living in submission to Christ as Lord. Jesus said, *"If*
you love me, you will obey my commands" (John 14:15). In fact, so
essential is repentance to true faith that Jesus cannot conceive
of one without the other: *"Anyone who loves me will obey my*
commands. Whoever does not love me does not keep my commands"
(John 14:23-24)

According to the New Testament, one of the key motivations for
repentance is to avoid the terrible wrath of God at the coming
judgment. Jesus declared to the Pharisees:

"Who warned you to flee from the coming wrath? Produce fruit in
keeping with repentance!" (Matthew 3:7).

Similarly, the Apostle Paul warned some of his readers:

"Because of your unrepentant heart, you are storing up wrath against yourselves for the day of wrath, when God's righteous judgment will be revealed" (Romans 2:5)

THE POP GOSPEL MESSAGE

It is this fundamental doctrine of repentance that is either entirely lacking or significantly obfuscated by the haze of sugar-coated language in the post-modern pop gospel. Diluted language is often employed, such as emphasising the fact that God gives us grace to make a fresh start, and that through Christ's indwelling presence we can leave our past mistakes behind and start again. The effect of this softer language subtly, yet profoundly, dilutes the message of the gospel. Christ is now viewed as the one who offers us a product; the ability to realign our lives so that we can achieve the fulfilment and purpose that has been missing so far. Our need to turn from our sins and make profound changes in our life in order to avoid the wrath of God is almost completely missing in pop gospel preaching.

An example of this kind of diluted gospel appears in Rick Warren's best-selling book, "The Purpose Driven Life". In his only explanation of the gospel within the entire book, he states:

"First believe, believe God loves you and made you for His purposes. Believe you're not an accident. Believe you were made to last forever. Believe God has chosen you to have a relationship with Jesus who died on the cross for you. Believe that no matter what you've done, God wants to forgive you. Second, receive Jesus into your life as your Lord and Saviour. Receive His forgiveness for your sins. Receive his Spirit, who will give you the power to fulfil your life purpose. The Bible says "Whoever believes and trusts the Son gets in on every-

thing, life complete and forever." Wherever you are reading this I invite you to bow your head and quietly whisper the prayer that will change your eternity: "Jesus, I believe in You and I receive You." If you sincerely meant that prayer, congratulations! Welcome to the family of God!" [1]

Did you notice a glaring omission in that outline of the gospel? Repentance is completely missing! He speaks of receiving God's offer of forgiveness but fails to mention what God demands of us in order to receive that forgiveness; repentance! According to Warren, all we have to do is believe in Jesus in order to receive all the goodies that he offers. We then *"get in on everything"* - an appalling translation of John 3:36.

This self-focused, diluted gospel is typical of the preaching of promoters of this pop gospel. John MacArthur, commenting on this kind of watered-down articulation of the gospel, states, *"That is an inadequate gospel. That is a gospel that will contribute to apostasy."* [2] MacArthur's point is that people who are not brought to repentance, will inevitably exhibit the shallow-rooted kind of commitment that Jesus described in the Parable of the Sower, and will eventually fall away.

Sadly, the ubiquitous influence of this watered-down pop gospel is evident in many conservative evangelical churches, as seen by the disproportionate preponderance of sermons focusing on positive aspects of faith, compared to the paucity of messages which refer, in any significant way, to repentance from sin. Repentance isn't easy to sell to a generation who want everything on their own terms – even salvation. This lack of any significant teaching about the need for repentance is reflected in the growing problem of sexual immorality which is in epidemic proportions in many youth groups and churches.

Acclaimed theologian, J.I. Packer, lamented this watering-down of the Gospel, when he stated:

"We have lost our grip on the biblical gospel. Without realising it, we have during the past century bartered that gospel for a substitute product which, though it looks similar enough in points of detail, is as a whole a decidedly different thing. Hence our troubles; for the substitute product does not answer the ends for which the authentic gospel has in past days proved itself so mighty.... One way of stating the difference between it and the old gospel is to say that it is too exclusively concerned to be 'helpful' to man – to bring peace, comfort, happiness, satisfaction – and too little concerned to glorify God." [3]

By seeking to make the gospel less offensive, purveyors of the pop gospel have promoted a brand of easy-believism, whereby what you believe makes few demands upon how you live. It promises much and asks for very little. This sugar-coated message may well have drawn more bees to the honey pot, but it has done so at the cost of the integrity of the gospel and, in all probability, at the cost of many people's true salvation.

14

WHAT ARE WE SAVED TO?

So far, we have examined the pop gospel's divergent answers to three questions; *"What is our intrinsic worth?"*, *"What are we saved from?"* and *"How are we saved?"*. In this chapter, we will examine the question, *"What are we saved to?"* This question can be re-phrased, *"Now that I'm saved, what now? What is my purpose?"* The pop gospel's divergent response to this question can be divided into two categories; differences of emphasis and differences of addition.

DIFFERENCES OF EMPHASIS

Both the biblical gospel and the modern pop gospel acknowledge certain benefits that accrue to the Christian; fulfilment, joy, a sense of purpose, answered prayer and God's peace, presence and strength. The pop gospel, however, places much more emphasis upon these benefits. Whereas the biblical gospel acknowledges them as side benefits to the central purpose of worshipping, obeying and serving God, the pop gospel has enthroned them as the centre-point of its message. J. I. Packer comments:

"One way of stating the difference between it [the new pop gospel] and the old gospel is to say that it is too exclusively concerned to be 'helpful' to man — to bring peace, comfort, happiness, satisfaction — and too little concerned to glorify God. The old gospel was 'helpful' too — more so, indeed, than is the new — but incidentally, for its first concern was always to give glory to God."[1]

In its desire to make the gospel as attractive as possible, the purveyors of the pop gospel have transformed the ***incidental benefits*** of the Christian life into its ***central focus.*** By contrast, the old gospel was extremely clear in indicating that the central purpose of the Christian life is to worship God, the twin components of which are obedience and service. As Christians, we live to worship and bring glory to God, through our obedience to him and our faithful, sacrificial service for his kingdom. As we do this, we will ***incidentally*** be the recipients of the fulfilled life that Jesus spoke of (John 10:10), but it is not to be our focus or our primary purpose for living. The intended focus of our lives is to love, obey and serve God, rather than seek our own fulfilment.

In essence, the contrasting emphases of the two gospels can be described as the worship of God vs the fulfilment of man. J.I. Packer comments:

"The centre of reference [of the old gospel] was unambiguously God. But in the new gospel the centre of reference is man. Whereas the chief aim of the old was to teach people to worship God, the concern of the new seems limited to making them feel better. The subject of the old gospel was God and his ways with men; the subject of the

new is man and the help God gives him. There is a world of differ-ence. The whole perspective and emphasis of gospel preaching has changed." [2]

DIFFERENCES OF ADDITION

In answering the question, *"Now that I'm saved, what now?",* the modern, self-focused pop gospel makes several extraordinary additional promises which were never part of the old, biblical gospel. These promises have the appearance of scriptural justi-fication but are, in fact, based upon poor exegesis, often ignoring both the contextual and lexical meaning of biblical passages. There are three unscriptural promises that are touted to prospective spiritual consumers; prosperity, universal healing and victory. I have discussed each of these in detail in my book, *"Making Sense of the Bible",* but include below a very brief overview of their unscriptural foundation:

1. **PROSPERITY.** This is the idea that God will bless Christians financially and positionally (i.e. success - rising to the top) if we are faithful. It is based upon several old covenant promises taken completely out of context (Malachi 3:9-10 and Jeremiah 29:11) as well as gross misinterpretations of several New Testa-ment passages such as Luke 6:38 and 2 Corinthians 9:6. This teaching completely ignores the fact that EVERY reference to wealth and money in the New Testament is in the form of a *warning* against wealth, often urging us to give our money and possessions away, and warning how difficult it is for the wealthy to enter the kingdom of heaven. Despite this, a plethora of modern preachers continue to lure people into their church pews with false promises of prosperity. The prosperity doctrine appeals to the greed and avarice of modern man and is a blight

upon the message of the true gospel. Rev Tim Costello, CEO of World Vision Australia, did not mince words on this issue when he said:

"The quickest way to degrade the gospel is to link it with money and the pursuit of money. It is the total opposite of what Jesus preached. These people have learnt nothing from the mistakes made by the American televangelists" (Sydney Morning Herald, 2007).

2. UNIVERSAL HEALING. This refers to the supposed promise that the Christian will now be healed of every disease all the time – that it is our rightful inheritance now, because Jesus purchased it on the cross for us. Once again, this misinterprets several biblical passages such as James 5:15, Matthew 8:17 and Isaiah 53:4-6, taking them completely out of context. (See my book, "Making Sense of the Bible" for a detailed analysis of these passages). This belief ignores the New Testament teaching that complete healing and deliverance from disease is our future inheritance (Revelation 21:4). While God certainly can and does heal people today, this is to be regarded as exceptional rather than normative, as evidenced by the ongoing sickness and lack of healing experienced by Paul (Galatians 4:13), Trophimus (2 Timothy 4:20) and Timothy (1 Timothy 5:23). Furthermore, it ignores the evidence of all the great saints throughout the ages, many of whom suffered ongoing debilitating, unhealed illnesses despite being used greatly by God.

3. VICTORY and SUCCESS. This is a nebulous, emotive concept, often incorporated into the pop gospel, which promises that God's miraculous power will now enable us to rise up and overcome all obstacles placed in our paths, so that we will be successful in all that we set our hearts and minds to do. The extreme version of this is the *"word of faith"* movement, which asserts that if we *"name it and claim it"* God will, indeed **must**, accede to our wishes and grant what we ask. A more moderate incarnation of this message has found its way into many evangelical churches. I recently listened to a sermon podcast, *"Choosing Your Future: 5 Crucial Choices To Unleash God's Plan For Your Life"*. Within a few minutes, the preacher was asserting that *"God wants you to be successful in your business ... in all of your life"*. He went on to expound the keys to unlocking God's power in your life so that you can achieve the success that God wants to give you.

This triumphalist message appears to be more hype than anything else. It is based very loosely upon a small number of scriptural passages which are taken completely out of context (eg. Jeremiah 29:11 and John 15:7). Jesus never promised his followers "success" in a worldly sense. Instead, he warned that his disciples would experience *"many troubles" (John 16:33)*. Rather than promising us victory over difficulties or deliverance from trials, the New Testament promises us God's strength and comfort **through** trials and difficulties (1 Peter 1:6; James 1:2; 2 Thessalonians 1:4; Luke 22:28; 2 Corinthians 1:4; Hebrews 12:4-13). The pop gospel's false triumphalism also completely ignores the experience of the Apostles and many of God's great saints throughout the ages who endured terrible trials, often eventuating in the loss of their lives for the sake of the gospel.

The sugar-coated false promises of the pop gospel are sweet music to the ears of modern man. They appeal to our self-focused natures – to our desire for a prosperous, healthy, successful life, free from the annoying problems that plague the rest of mankind. Churches that proclaim these false promises will almost certainly attract more people to sit in their pews and put money in their offering buckets. Unfortunately, these are hollow promises, and tend to produce the "revolving door" syndrome in such churches. Jim Reiher, in his book, *"The Eye Of The Needle"*, writes:

"A lot of sheep are wandering away from the flock when the simplistic promises of prosperity teachers are not fulfilled in their lives. They suffer unnecessary emotional, spiritual and economic hardship, because they try to implement the principles of success and prosperity and are disappointed".[3]

We would do well to heed the words of 2 Timothy 4:3-5, which warn us:

"For the time will come when people will not put up with sound doctrine. Instead, to suit their own desires, they will gather around them a great number of teachers to say what their itching ears want to hear. They will turn aside to myths. But you, keep your head in all situations, endure hardship ... discharge all the duties of your ministry." (2 Timothy 4:3-5)

15

THE CURSE OF THE SHALLOW SERMON

I am not a grumpy old man who bemoans the modern world and hankers after the "good old days" when things were much better. (At least, I don't think I am, but perhaps my wife might have a different opinion!) However, I have lived long enough to witness a significant shift in the content and style of preaching in churches. Sermons in churches which preach the pop gospel have become shorter, simpler, shallower, more repetitive, less theological and more inclined to focus upon the psychological and emotional needs of the listeners rather than focus on Christ.

This shift is particularly obvious when one compares the average sermon today with the sermons of the great preachers of the past, such as George Whitfield, Charles Spurgeon, Alexander Campbell, R.C. Sproul, Alexander Maclaren, D. Martyn Lloyd-Jones, Matthew Henry, J.C. Ryle, John Wesley, John Calvin and D.L. Moody. These sermons were deeply theological, complex and Christ-centred. They also treated the

Bible differently. The Bible was used as the source text upon which the message was based, rather than as an illustrative text to support the preacher's desired message. The sermons of old were often expositional, based upon verse by verse explanation of the biblical text. Listeners were required to think deeply. By comparison, in many churches today, the sermon often glosses over the surface of a Bible passage, merely using it as a spring-board into the preacher's topic, rather than properly exegeting the passage and delving deeply into its meaning.

I recently listened to a podcast sermon, supposedly based upon John 17. This is the prayer of Jesus as he prays for his disciples and for all who will follow him. This Bible passage is filled with marvellous theological truths:

-The irresistible grace of God (vv. 6, 24)

-The Lordship of Christ over all humanity (v.2)

-The eternal existence of the Son (vv.5, 24)

-The nature and ontological order of the Trinity (vv.1, 4, 5, 7, 8, 10-12, 18, 21-26)

-The defining characteristics of salvation (v.3)

-The crucial nature of Christian unity (vv.11, 20-23,

-The serious reality of spiritual warfare (vv.11, 15)

-The inevitability of suffering and persecution (v.14)

-The sovereignty and of God - evident in Judas' betrayal of Jesus as a fulfilment of prophecy (v.12)

-God's pre-election of the saints from eternity – (vv. 6, 9, 12)

-The relationship between sanctification and knowledge of the Truth (vv.17, 19)

-The mission of the church (v.18)

-The certainty of eternal salvation (v.24)

-The indwelling of Christ within the believer (vv.21-23-26)

Sadly, the preacher did not mention any of these incredibly profound truths. He ignored **all** these marvellous truths, saying *"There is so much in this passage that I don't have time to go into"*. Instead, he gave a three-point sermon:

1. Prayer is a dialogue, not a monologue (a point which **cannot** be made from this passage, because Jesus' prayer in this passage **WAS** a monologue! What appalling exegesis!)
2. Jesus had an intimate relationship with the Father (which the preacher compared to his close, yet flawed, relationship with his own son)
3. We are invited into the same intimate relationship with the Father

While points 2 and 3 are not wrong, they constitute an incredibly superficial exegesis of this profound passage! If I could meet with that preacher I would ask him, *"If you didn't have time to go into all those other profound truths, when will you have time? Will you ever come back to that passage and expound those incredibly profound doctrines? Why did you choose not to speak about them this time and, instead, speak about things that **aren't even in that passage**?"* Sadly, this kind of shallow exegesis is typical of much of the preaching within today's church, because preachers are scared of boring seekers with doctrine. I also suspect that many preachers exist at a very superficial theological level, themselves, and are much more comfortable paddling in the shallows.

The style and content of the modern sermon is significantly different to sermons from only 50 years ago. Obviously, some changes in grammar and vocabulary are inevitable in response to the ongoing evolution of language, but this is mere window-dressing. The changes that concern me are more profound and deeply disturbing. In a previous chapter I discussed one of those profound changes – the influence of pop psychology upon the proclamation of the gospel, resulting in a focus upon the concepts of self-esteem, self-fulfilment and relationships. A second, equally disturbing trend has been what I describe as the dumbing down of the sermon. Today's sermons are, on the whole, much more simplistic than in previous eras, and are generally pitched at an intellectual level of about 12 years of age.

This has come about as a result of the hugely influential "*Seeker Friendly Church*" movement, started in the United States by Robert Schuller and subsequently spear-headed by Bill Hybels (Willow Creek Community Church) and, more recently, by Rick Warren (Saddleback Community Church). The Seeker Friendly movement has profoundly influenced almost every church in the western world. Basically, the seeker friendly church tries to reach out to the unsaved person by making the church experience as comfortable, inviting, and non-threatening as possible. The idea behind the concept is to get as many unsaved people through the doors as possible. Key elements include a hot band, snappy technology, a good creche and an effective kids program. The sermon, in particular, has been radically transformed by this movement. In order to appeal to outsiders, sermons are shorter, simpler and focused on self-improvement, fulfilment, success, marriage, relationships, communication and a myriad of other "practical" topics that are appealing to modern ears.

The seeker friendly church is a consumer driven church that regards the gospel as a product to be marketed, with tarted-up packaging to make it attractive to the consumer. For example, Bill Hybels, who used to be the Senior Pastor of Willow Creek Community Church before he was dismissed for sexual indiscretion, had a sign on his door which read, *"What is our business? Who is our customer? What does the customer consider value?"*[1] That says it all!

While the seeker sensitive movement has had widespread influence upon the general style of modern-day church services, its most significant impact has been upon the content of the sermon. Preachers of today are taught the KISS principle: Keep It Simple Stupid. Sermons are pitched at a much simpler, shallower level. Repetition abounds. Points are ponderously developed. Illustrations have become the foundation of the message, with the Bible used to provide occasional support. Seeker friendly sermons avoid those aspects of the Bible that are offensive to outsiders or considered to be too cerebral or theological. Consequently, it has been estimated that once a person has attended church for approximately 3 years, they have learned everything that they will ever learn from the sermons. Every message from then on will be a repeat of the same simple themes with slightly different packaging.

Preacher and Bible Scholar, John MacArthur, laments this "dumbing down" of the sermon, referring to it as "condescending"[2]. He's right. It treats people as though they are idiots. This "dumbing down" of the sermon has had profound consequences within Christianity. Churches are now full of people who have not progressed beyond the basics (and even these basics have often been distorted and sugar-coated).

Several years ago, Willow Creek Community Church undertook a multiple year study of the effectiveness of its seeker friendly services. It interviewed and surveyed church members to investigate the spiritual maturity of its congregation and their satisfaction with the seeker friendly program. The results were damning. The final report indicated a serious lack of spiritual maturity amongst the congregation, including an appallingly shallow understanding of the Bible. It also revealed a strong desire amongst the congregation for deeper, meatier teaching, together with a general dissatisfaction with the shallow nature of Sunday sermons.

Bill Hybels, the former senior pastor of Willow Creek, while speaking at a subsequent leadership summit, confessed:

"We made a mistake. What we should have done when people crossed the line of faith and become Christians, we should have started teaching people that they have to take responsibility to become self-feeders. We should have gotten people, taught people, how to read their Bible between services, how to do the spiritual practices much more aggressively on their own."[3]

This frank confession, together with the disturbing findings of the Willow Creek church report, sent shock waves throughout Christendom. Sadly, many churches today are continuing blindly down the seeker friendly path, offering a watered-down version of the gospel that has already proven to be ineffective in producing mature disciples of Christ.

The writer to the Hebrews lamented a similar lack of spiritual maturity within some of the churches throughout the dispersia:

"Although by this time you ought to be teachers, you need someone to re-teach you the basic principles of God's word. You need milk, not solid food! Everyone who lives on milk is still an infant, inexperienced in the message of righteousness. But solid food is for the mature, who by constant use have trained their sensibilities to distinguish good from evil...." (Hebrews 5:12-13)

A couple of years ago I conducted a mid-week course called "Deepening Your Faith". It was held one night each week for ten weeks and consisted of a one-hour talk followed by questions and answers. I dealt with weighty doctrinal topics that don't get much airplay in Sunday services – including biblical inspiration and inerrancy, Bible manuscripts and variants, the two covenants, progressive revelation, interpreting the Bible Christologically and developing a clear, biblical theology of suffering. The pastor of that church thought we might get a dozen or so people interested in pursuing this kind of weighty teaching. Instead, we got 65 participants who turned up enthusiastically week after week. They expressed great joy at being able to study these kinds of theological issues at depth. They also expressed a desire that Sunday sermons should deal with biblical issues at greater depth. Subsequent to that first course, I ran a further three mid-week courses at the same church, all with similar weighty content, and all similarly well-attended. Throughout these courses I was regularly asked, *"Why don't we learn these sorts of things in church?"* To be fair, the church in question has quite sound biblical teaching most Sundays. There is usually nothing wrong with what it teaches. It's just that it is pitched at a very simplistic level and doesn't often go beyond the basics.

There is a hunger among Christians for meaty biblical teaching, and a general dissatisfaction with the simplified messages of our seeker-friendly pulpits. Preachers who deliberately avoid dealing with complex doctrinal issues in their sermons should consider the Bible's plea for Christians to be growing in knowledge and depth of insight;

"Make every effort to add to your faith, virtue, and to add to virtue, knowledge" (2 Peter 1:5)

"And this is my prayer for you, that your love may abound more and more in knowledge and depth of insight" (Philippians 1:9)

These verses indicate that both head and heart are important in our faith. Love needs to be more than mere shallow emotion; it needs to *"abound more and more in knowledge and depth of insight"*. This infers continual growth in our knowledge and understanding of the deeper things of God's Word.

Are you continually growing in your own knowledge of God and of salvation? Is the preaching in your church substantial and meaty? Does it tackle the complex theological issues of faith? Does it deal at depth with biblical truth? Are you regularly learning new things? Or are you hearing the same kind of simplistic messages over and over again? Do you feel like you've heard it all before?

Maybe that's because you have.

16

FOUNDATIONAL FLAWS OF THE SEEKER FRIENDLY MOVEMENT

The seeker-friendly or seeker-sensitive church movement, epitomised by Willow Creek Community Church and Saddleback Community Church and adopted by tens of thousands of churches world-wide, seeks to gear its services to the unsaved by making them attractive, non-threatening, entertaining and relevant to their perceived needs. It is a consumer driven approach to church, employing savvy marketing strategies and preaching an appealing, modified gospel.

Apart from the generally shallow and misleading content of its sermons, the movement is also based upon several foundational philosophies which are deeply flawed. I briefly outline several of these flawed presuppositions below:

1. UNBELIEVERS ARE SEEKING GOD

The seeker-friendly movement assumes that there is a swathe of people out there who are earnestly seeking God, and that our old fashioned services are the problem: our out-dated way of "doing church" is the stumbling block stopping these earnest seekers from finding God. The Bible, however, paints a very different picture. There are no true seekers: no-one is naturally and earnestly searching for God!

David, in Psalm 14:2-3 states it plainly:

"The LORD has looked down from heaven upon the sons of men, to see if there are any who understand, who seek after God. They have all turned aside, together they have become corrupt; There is no one who does good, not even one." (See also Psalm 53:2-3).

Paul echoes these words in Romans 3:10-11:

"There is no one righteous, not even one. There is no one who understands. There is no one who seeks God."

The Bible portrays unbelievers, not as those who earnestly seek God, but rather as spiritually dead (Colossians 2:13), spiritually rebellious (Ephesians 2:1-3), and spiritually hard-hearted (Ephesians 4:18). Even though God's self-disclosure through nature and our consciences should cause men to seek Him (Acts 17:27-29), unbelievers have rejected the truth that they know, becoming *"futile in their thoughts so that their foolish hearts were darkened" (Rom. 1:21).*

In other words, the reason unbelievers are not flocking to our services is not because we are doing it wrong, but because of their hard hearts! People are not seeking God; it is God's Spirit who draws them to himself.

2. EVERYTHING IN A SERVICE MUST BE UNDERSTANDABLE TO UNBELIEVERS

One of the strongest foundational philosophies of seeker-friendly churches is that everything within the service must be understandable to unbelievers – everything must be pitched at their level. According to this philosophy, complex doctrine, creeds and weighty theological concepts have no place in Sunday services. The philosophy is that that kind of meaty content needs to be dealt with in mid-week meetings for Christians: the Sunday service is for unbelievers.

The problem with this is that the Bible says:

"The natural person does not accept the things of the Spirit of God, for they are folly to him, and he is not able to understand them because they are spiritually discerned" (1 Corinthians 2:14 ESV).

In other words, the reason unsaved people, when they first come to church, may not understand the things that are said and sung, is not that we've pitched it too high for them, it's because they are spiritually dead. If we adopt the policy of dumbing down the service to a level where unbelievers will understand, we will need to basically remove almost everything of any significant spiritual content! Which is exactly what seeker-friendly churches do!

In so doing, these churches fail to trust in the work of God's Spirit to open the minds of unbelievers – a work that He and He alone can do. It takes a miracle for an unbeliever to comprehend spiritual truth, but such miracles happen very often, otherwise there would be no Christians!

The dumbing down of church services also has the dire consequence of failing to provide adequate teaching and training for Christians. By failing to provide meat, and only feeding people milk, the seeker-friendly church produces spiritual babies who never grow up to maturity. Additionally, the problem with relying on church members to attend extra mid-week meetings in order to receive deeper teaching is that many church members only come on a Sunday, and so they will never get anything other than the basics.

3. THE GOSPEL NEEDS RE-PACKAGING TO APPEAL TO UNBELIEVERS

The seeker-friendly movement seeks to modify and re-package the gospel in order to make it appealing and relevant to unbelievers. It removes or avoids many of the so-called negative aspects of the gospel such as sin, judgment, hell, God's wrath, the total depravity of mankind and our need for repentance. In so doing it hopes to sell the gospel as an attractive proposition. According to this philosophy, the reason the church throughout the ages has been relatively unsuccessful in evangelising the world is that we have been too negative. Apparently, Paul and the other Apostles got it wrong when they spoke so much about sin and repentance!

The problem with this philosophy is that the Bible clearly indicates that the gospel will always seem foolish to unbelievers – until and unless God's Spirit works in their hearts to bring them to faith. Consider these verses:

"The message of the cross is foolishness to those who are perishing ..." (1 Corinthians 1:18)

"But we preach Christ crucified, a stumbling block to the Jews and foolishness to Gentiles ..." (1 Corinthians 1:23)

Notice that while Paul concedes that the gospel appears foolish to unbelievers, he doesn't stop preaching it and he doesn't seek to dress it up or modify it.

In other words, the problem is not in the message, it's in the hearts of the recipients. Our job is not to change the message, but to pray for God's Spirit to change their hearts.

4. CHURCHES REQUIRE CLEVER MARKETING IN ORDER TO GROW

Another philosophical foundation of seeker-friendly churches is that the church requires clever marketing in order to be attractive and effective. Powerful, emotive music is played, clever drama is sometimes performed, mood lighting is used, impressive audio visuals are projected, creche is provided, good coffee is served, a polished welcoming team is there to assist – all to make the unbeliever comfortable, to make their experience of church enjoyable and to convince them to return. According to this philosophy, churches that don't market the gospel successfully like this are "out of date" and will gradually become ineffective.

Of course, there is nothing wrong with any of these practical procedures and ministries in themselves. They can be quite helpful in enhancing the experience of worship and ministering effectively to church members and visitors alike. But when too much emphasis is placed upon these kind of extraneous frills, a church can subtly drift into a consumerist mentality, where the predominant philosophy of the leaders is *"How can we sell our product better?"* and the predominant attitude of those attending is *"What's in it for me? Are my needs being met?"* In this kind of church, it is easy to begin to place one's confidence in clever marketing strategies and product placement, rather than in the inherent power of the gospel to transform lives (Romans 1:16). In 1 Corinthians 2:1-5, the Apostle Paul writes of his visit to Corinth and stresses that he deliberately avoided "dressing up" the gospel in order to make it more appealing. Paul was convinced that the gospel didn't need any help from him:

"And so it was with me, brothers and sisters. When I came to you, I did not come with eloquence or human wisdom as I proclaimed to you the testimony about God. For I resolved to know nothing while I was with you except Jesus Christ and him crucified. I came to you in weakness with great fear and trembling. My message and my preaching were not with wise and persuasive words, but with a demonstration of the Spirit's power, so that your faith might not rest on human wisdom, but on God's power." (1 Cor 2:1-5)

In other words, Paul deliberately did not use showy techniques or clever strategies to impress his listeners. He had such faith in the inherent power of the gospel that he let it speak for itself, so that the result was true conversion through God's power rather than garnering superficial followers through his own cleverness. Elsewhere, Paul declares his absolute confidence in the power of the gospel alone to save:

"I am not ashamed of the gospel, for it is the power of God for the salvation of everyone who believes ..." (Romans 1:16)

5. NUMBERS ARE A RELIABLE MEASURE OF SUCCESS

The seeker-friendly movement believes that numbers are the ultimate measure of success. A church that is truly effective will be growing numerically.

While it is true that the church's mission on earth is to *"make disciples of all nations" (Matthew 28:19-20)*, and that this should be reflected in more people turning to Christ in faith and repentance, two key points need to be noted.

Firstly, numerical growth is not a reliable means of assessing effectiveness. The number of bottoms on pews does not automatically equate to true church growth. A church with great music, great coffee, entertaining sermons and an overall glitzy performance may attract large numbers of pew sitters who are never truly converted and who are there for all the wrong reasons. Jesus encountered this very issue when he rebuked the large crowd who had followed him only because they had come for a free lunch! (John 6:26-27). Conversely, low or shrinking numbers are not necessarily an indication of ineffectiveness. Jesus modelled this himself when, during the latter part of his ministry, we are told that his non-seeker-friendly message actually drove the crowds away! (John 6:53-66. For example, verse 66 says, *"From this time, many of his disciples turned back and no longer followed him."*). One could hardly accuse Jesus of being ineffective! Numbers, by themselves, are an extremely unreliable means of assessing true spiritual effectiveness.

Secondly, focusing on numbers has an inherent danger. Numerical growth can become the primary goal, the thing that drives everything a church does, rather than true spiritual growth. In such a church, anything that puts more bottoms on pews becomes justifiable, without any further need to evaluate its biblical validity or its ultimate spiritual consequence. Churches driven by the need for continual numerical growth can easily stray into worldly strategies and clever marketing ploys that produce superficial results, but which can undermine the gospel and cause great harm to the spiritual health of the church.

Charles Spurgeon, the powerful preacher of the 19th century "Great Awakening", once preached a sermon entitled, *"Feeding Sheep or Amusing Goats?"*, in which he said;

"An evil is in the professed camp of the Lord, so gross in its impudence, that the most short-sighted can hardly fail to notice it during the past few years. It has developed at an abnormal rate, even for evil. It has worked like leaven until the whole lump ferments. The devil has seldom done a cleverer thing than hinting to the church that part of their mission is to provide entertainment for the people, with a view to winning them."

It is important to clarify, here, that I am not opposed to modernising church services and streamlining church practices in order to make them more relevant to the 21st century. Technology, lighting, drama and music can all play a part in enhancing services and enabling them to have a greater impact. Having a well-organised welcoming team, a good quality creche and appealing morning tea facilities also help make visitors and regulars feel welcome and cared for. There is nothing wrong with any of these things. Nor is there anything wrong with praying for and working towards numerical growth through conversion. Indeed, the salvation of the lost is at the heart of the church's mission.

The problem arises, however, when a church develops such a ravenous desire for numerical growth that it will do anything to achieve it. In the case of many seeker-friendly churches, this has involved a radically altered gospel and an over-reliance on superficial window dressing to attract more consumers.

Are you a member of such a church? Why not give your leadership a copy of this book? Why not start a dialogue with them? If that proves unfruitful, perhaps it's time to look for a church that faithfully proclaims the gospel and relies on the power of God rather than the cleverness of man.

17

RESPONDING TO THE POP GOSPEL

I n this chapter, I want to address the question, *"How should we respond to the proliferation of the pop gospel within the modern church?"* In other words, what can be done about it? What can I do if I am in a church where this kind of message is the norm?

EXHORTATION TO PASTORS

We who are preachers need to be reminded that we have been given a great responsibility. James 3:1 says:

"Not many of you should become teachers, my brethren, because you know that we who teach will be judged more strictly."

That is an incredibly sobering truth. It reminds pastors that it is not your church; it is God's. And he has placed you there to teach his people *his* message; not *your* message. Not a modified message. His message. Any Sunday when we stand in the pulpit or lectern to speak, we are called to speak God's unadulterated gospel of truth and grace, trusting that it is *"God's power for the salvation of everyone who believes" (Romans 1:16)*, and resisting the temptation to change it or dress it up in order to make it more appealing. It is a temptation that needs to be resisted continually and vigorously, because our hearts are deceitful above all else and the temptation is great – the temptation to soft-sell the gospel in order to improve our results. Guard your heart. Immerse yourself in God's Word. Be diligent in prayer. Seek the counsel and support of wise fellow preachers. Ask someone to occasionally evaluate your sermons. And in everything;

"Do your best to present yourself to God as one approved, a worker who does not need to be ashamed and who correctly handles the word of truth." (2 Timothy 2:15)

EXHORTATION TO CHURCH MEMBERS

Are you a member of a church? Although you may not be a preacher, you still have a role to play in the preaching that takes place in your church.

Your first responsibility is to practise discernment. You are not meant to passively accept everything that is said from the pulpit and assume that it has been handed down directly from heaven. Preachers are fallible. We make mistakes. We don't always get it right. You ought to have a Bible in front of you every Sunday morning so that you can check the Bible verses for yourself, reading the verses around them to make sure they have not been taken out of context or misquoted. You are meant to listen with a discerning ear, in order to sift truth from error, so that you will not be led astray.

In speaking about the need to discern between false and true prophets, Paul writes:

"Test them all; hold on to what is good and reject every kind of evil" (1 *Thessalonians 5:21).*

Similarly, John writes:

"Do not believe every spirit, but test the spirits to see whether they are from God, because many false prophets have gone out into the world ..." (1 John 4:1).

You are called to be discerning. Luke records that when the Apostle Paul preached in Berea, the believers did not accept his teaching unthinkingly, but continually evaluated it against the scriptures to ensure that he was speaking the truth:

"Now the Bereans were of more noble character than the Thessalonians, for they received the message with great eagerness and examined the Scriptures every day to see if what Paul said was true" (Acts 17:11)

The Bible calls us all to emulate the Bereans. We are not meant to passively and unthinkingly accept everything that is preached in our church. Pastors and preachers are not infallible; they sometimes err. The mature Christian is one who listens with an open Bible and a discerning mind. You are called to test everything against God's Word, not in order to catch your pastor out, but to protect yourself and your church from drifting into error.

Your second responsibility is to pray for the preacher! Are you guilty of whining and complaining about the preaching without actually praying for the preacher? Do you believe in the power of prayer? If you and others in your church have concerns about the faithfulness to the gospel and to God's Word of those who preach, your first response should be to pray for God to work in their hearts and to change them from within.

Your third responsibility is to speak to the preacher/s and voice your concerns. The modern preacher / pastor has, in many churches, been placed on a pedestal and removed from immediate accountability from their flock. People feel that it is not their right to question or criticise what is taught from the pulpit. That is simply not true. It *is* your right. In fact, it is your responsibility. Your allegiance is to God and His Word, and this must take priority over your natural desire to not offend your pastor. If you have genuine concerns that those who preach are not proclaiming the gospel completely or accurately, then you need to be willing to sit down with them, with an open Bible, and respectfully voice your concerns. If they are mature Christians, they should at least listen to your concerns and take them seriously. In fact, their response will tell you a lot about their true character.

A preacher who is consistently misrepresenting the gospel will almost certainly not change if he or she is never challenged. But if enough people speak up and voice a similar concern, at the very least it will cause them to be more circumspect as they prepare their messages, knowing that there are people who are listening carefully and who are concerned about the content. Even the most stubborn preacher cannot help but be influenced by the knowledge that his or her sermons are being carefully weighed and analysed in the light of the Scriptures.

Of course, if all this fails and the gospel continues to be compromised in your church, the question has to be asked, *"Can I continue to sit under this teaching?"* As a younger Christian

I faced this exact issue in a church where the preacher had very little idea of the biblical gospel and dished up a weekly, sloppy diet of love messages. After several people met with him on several occasions to discuss his content with no resulting improvement, my fiancé (now my wife) and I decided that we had to leave. It was not an easy decision, because we had many good friends in that church. But we recognised that if we continued to subject ourselves to that kind of watered-down, sugar-coated gospel, it would inevitably affect us spiritually.

The self-centred, watered-down, sugar-coated pop gospel has become entrenched within the Western church. It has resulted in churches filled with people who have little understanding of God's Word and of the true message of the gospel. The pop gospel, by avoiding the unpleasant concepts of the seriousness of sin and the need for repentance, may well have attracted more people to sit in church pews, but their depth of commitment and the genuineness of their conversion must be seriously questioned. The slippery-tongued purveyors of false promises will one day be held to account for their distortion of the truth.

God is calling his church to return to the unadorned, pure proclamation of the true gospel. He is calling pastors and preachers to give up their infatuation with post-modern window dressing, and trust in the inherent power of the gospel to transform lives.

Prominent Bible teacher, John MacArthur, Jr. tells of an interesting experience he had in witnessing to an unbelieving Jewish doctor. MacArthur's simple evangelistic 'tactic' was to give the man a copy of the Gospel of John. He stated:

"The Bible is like a lion. You don't have to defend it. Just open the door and let it out. It'll take care of itself."

MacArthur then continued his story:

"The next Friday I received a telephone call. The doctor wanted to see me again.... He sat down on the couch, dropped the Bible beside him, and said, "I know who He is." I said, "You do?" He said, "Yes I do." I asked, "Who is He?" He replied, "I'll tell you one thing - He's not just a man." I said, "Really? Who is He?" He said, "He is God!" ... I asked, "You, a Jew, are telling me that Jesus Christ is God? How do you know that?" He said, "It's clear. It's right here in the Gospel of John." (Our Sufficiency in Christ, Dallas: Word, 1991, p. 143.)

David Wells cuts to the heart of the matter when he writes:

"Does the Church have the courage to become relevant by becoming biblical? Is it willing to break with the cultural habits of the time and propose something quite absurd, like recovering both the word and the meaning of sin? ... Why should the postmodern world believe the gospel when the Church appears so unsure of its truth that it dresses up that gospel in the garments of modernity to heighten its interest? ... We need the faith of the ages, not the reconstructions of a therapeutically driven and commercially inspired faith. And we need it, not least, because without it our postmodern world will become starved for the Word of God." ("Losing Our Virtue", Grand Rapids: Eerdmans, 1998; pp. 199, 207, 209.)

What about you? God calls each one of us to stand up for his truth in whatever location and whatever role he has placed us in. May God give you the strength to speak up for the truth, so that one day you will hear him say: *"Well done, good and faithful servant." (Matthew 25:23)*

18

ONCE SAVED, ALWAYS SAVED?

I n this final chapter, I want to provide a detailed exposé of the doctrine commonly referred to as "once saved, always saved." Extreme Calvinists promote this unfortunate belief, referring to it as *"the eternal security of the believer"* or the *"perseverance of the saints"*. This doctrine teaches that it is impossible for a Christian to fall away and lose their salvation. It is based on the belief that grace is unconditional; that once a person has been forgiven through Christ, their ongoing salvation is assured, regardless of the way they choose to live their life subsequently. Nothing they do or fail to do, no matter how consistently disobedient their life may become, can cause them to lose their salvation.

The Westminster Confession adopted by most Presbyterian churches, states:

"They whom God hath accepted in his Beloved, effectually called and sanctified by his Spirit, can neither totally nor finally fall away from the state of grace; but shall certainly persevere therein to the end, and

be eternally saved ... Nevertheless they may, through the temptations of Satan ... fall into grievous sins..." (Book of Confessions of the United Presbyterian Church, 1967 Ed., Sec. 6.086-6.088).

The Philadelphia Confession, adopted by many Baptist churches, is almost identical to the above.

Sam Morris, Pastor of the First Baptist Church, Stamford, Texas, expressed the doctrine in its most extreme form as follows:

"We take the position that a Christian's sins do not damn his soul! The way a Christian lives, what he says, his character, his conduct, or his attitude toward other people have nothing whatever to do with the salvation of his soul ... All the prayers a man may pray, all the Bibles he may read, all the churches he may belong to, all the services he may attend, all the sermons he may practice, all the debts he may pay, all the ordinances he may observe, all the laws he may keep, all the benevolent acts he may perform will not make his soul one whit safer; and all the sins he may commit from idolatry to murder will not make his soul in any more danger ... The way a man lives has nothing whatever to do with the salvation of his soul." (Morris, A Discussion Which Involves a Subject Pertinent to All Men, pp. 1,2; via Handbook of Religious Quotations, p. 24)

This is an appealing concept. Wouldn't it be comforting to think that nothing I could do or not do would jeopardise my salvation? However, if this doctrine is *not* true, then it would be a very dangerous doctrine because it would give people a false sense of security. People would not be on their guard against sin, and may not see any need to repent of ongoing sins, if they thought they would still be saved eternally despite any subsequent actions.

In this chapter I will demonstrate that this doctrine is refuted by the clear teaching of Scripture. The New Testament is replete with warnings against *"falling away"* (Hebrews 3:6-14; 4:9-11, 10:26-39), as well as assertions that only *"the one who stands firm to the end will be saved"* (Matthew 24:13). Jesus also warned *"If you do not remain in me, you are like a branch that is thrown away and withers; such branches are picked up, thrown into the fire and burned"* (John 15:6).

Two verses, in particular, have propped up the false doctrine of "once saved, always saved". Firstly, Romans 11:29.

"God's gifts and his call are irrevocable." (Romans 11:29)

This is a verse that is wrongly applied to personal salvation. Romans 11 is not speaking about personal salvation at this point. Romans 11 is describing the temporary apostasy of Israel and the fact that God will, toward the end of human history, cause the nation of Israel to finally accept Jesus as their Messiah. Although the nation of Israel does not currently accept Christ, its current unbelief will not last forever. God's *"call"* upon the nation of Israel to be his special people has not been rescinded. Those Jews who will be alive immediately before the second coming of Christ will finally turn to him in faith and repentance, and at that time *"all Israel will be saved"* (Romans 11:26).

This is God's wonderful promise for the nation of Israel, and this is what is meant by the assertion that "God's gifts and his call are irrevocable". The call that is being spoken of is God's call to the whole nation of Israel to be his chosen people. The "gifts" that are referred to are God's gifts of the prophets and the covenant that he gave to them. None of this will be rescinded, because in the end, God will ensure that the Jews finally acknowledge the Messiah that God sent to them, and they will be enfolded back into the people of God. This verse simply cannot be interpreted to mean that an individual Christian cannot lose their salvation!

The second verse that has propped up the "once saved, always saved" viewpoint is John 10:28.

"I give them eternal life, and they shall never perish; no one will snatch them out of my hand." (John 10:28)

In interpreting any verse of scripture, it is vital that we don't extrapolate it further than it is intended. And the best way of ensuring this, is to interpret a single verse such as this with the overwhelming weight of scripture elsewhere. In this case, there is a large body of scripture that describes either the conditional nature of one's ongoing salvation or the possible loss of salvation. I have already discussed many of these verses during the course of this book, but for the purposes of being exhaustive, let us list some of them again:

"Remain in me, and I will remain in you ... If you do not remain in me, you are like a branch that is thrown away and withers; such branches are picked up, thrown into the fire and burned." (John 15:6)

"If you continue in my word, then are you my disciples indeed." (John 8:31)

"Once you were alienated from God and were enemies in your minds because of your evil behaviour. But now he has reconciled you by Christ's physical body through death to present you holy in his sight, without blemish and free from accusation if you continue in your faith." (Colossians 1:21-23)

"Hold on to your faith and a good conscience, which some have now rejected and <u>have shipwrecked their faith</u>." (1 Timothy 1:19)

"Therefore, my beloved, as you have always obeyed, not as in my presence only, but now much more in my absence, <u>work out your own salvation with fear and trembling</u>." (Philippians 2:12)

"Therefore, my brothers and sisters, <u>make every effort to confirm your calling and election. For if you do these things</u>, you will never stumble, and you will receive a rich welcome into the eternal kingdom of our Lord and Saviour Jesus Christ." (2 Peter 1:10-11)

"Now I would remind you, brothers, of the gospel I preached to you, which you received, in which you stand, and by which you are being saved, <u>if you hold fast to the word I preached to you</u>—unless you believed in vain." (1 Corinthians 15:1-2)

"Consider therefore the kindness and sternness of God: sternness to those who fell, but kindness to you, <u>provided that you continue in his kindness. Otherwise, you also will be cut off</u>." (Romans 11:22)

"The one who endures to the end will be saved." (Matthew 24:13)

Can you see the conditional nature of salvation that is explicit in these verses? You will be saved in the end, **only** if you persevere until the end. Indeed, as we have noted in earlier chapters of this book, the scriptures are very clear that it is possible to be saved and then to lose that salvation: it is possible to receive God's grace and then fall away from it.

"You are severed from Christ, you who would be justified by the law; <u>you have fallen away from grace</u>." (Galatians 5:4)

"It is impossible for those who have once been enlightened, who have

tasted the heavenly gift, who have shared in the Holy Spirit, who have tasted the goodness of the word of God and the powers of the coming age and <u>who have fallen away</u>, to be brought back to repentance. To their loss they are crucifying the Son of God all over again and subjecting him to public disgrace." (Hebrews 6:4-6)

"If they have escaped the corruption of the world by knowing our Lord and Saviour Jesus Christ and are again entangled in it and are overcome, they are worse off at the end than they were at the beginning." (2 Peter 2:20)

Even the great Apostle Paul does not exempt himself from the possibility of falling away if he does not remain vigilant:

"But I discipline my body and keep it under control, lest after preaching to others I myself should be disqualified." (1 Cor 9:27)

This is the overwhelming testimony of scripture. It is, indeed, possible to lose one's salvation. Hebrews 6:4-6 is particularly clear. It describes people *"who have once been enlightened, who have tasted the heavenly gift, who have shared in the Holy Spirit, who have tasted the goodness of the word of God and the powers of the coming age and who have fallen away"*. Make no mistake about it: the people being described in this Hebrews passage were *definitely* once genuine Christians *and now are not*. The interpretive gymnastics required to claim that these people were not really Christians in the first place defies all accepted rules of hermeneutics (principles of biblical interpretation) and ignores the clear meaning of the passage.

So, what are we to make of the statement by Jesus that we mentioned at the beginning of this discourse?

"I give them eternal life, and they shall never perish; no one will snatch them out of my hand." (John 10:28)

How do we interpret this verse in a way that does not contradict the vast weight of other scriptures that clearly speak of the possibility of falling away? For the Bible does not contradict itself.

There is, in fact, a very simple explanation. No one can snatch you out of Christ's hand, but you can deliberately choose to step out of his hand yourself. By your wilful disobedience to his commands and your unwillingness to abide by his Lordship over your life, you can step out of Christ's hand yourself. Christ promises to protect you from anyone and anything that would seek to steal your salvation and take you away from God, but he does not promise to continue to save you if, by your actions, you show that you do not want to be saved. Christ will not save you against your will. If, at some point in the future, you reject his Lordship by refusing to abide by his commands anymore, he will let you go. If you show by your rebellious actions that you have turned your back on him, he will turn his back on you. He will not hold on to someone who does not want to be held on to. God does not drag people kicking and screaming into heaven.

The book of Hebrews arguably provides the most powerful proof against the misleading, "once saved, always saved" doctrine. In chapter 3, the writer reminds his readers of Israel's unfaithfulness to God. Despite the fact that they were God's chosen people, they hardened their hearts and rebelled against God. As a result, the entire generation of Israelites who rebelled at that time were subject to God's judgment and died in the wilderness, never seeing the land that God had promised them (Hebrews 3:7-11). These were God's own people, yet they fell from grace and were judged, losing their salvation.

Then, in the verse that immediately follows this historical lesson, the writer states:

"See to it, brothers and sisters, that none of you has a sinful, unbelieving heart leading you to turn away from the living God. But encourage one another daily, as long as it is called "Today," so that none of you may be hardened by sin's deceitfulness. We have come to share in Christ, if indeed we hold our original conviction firmly to the very end." (Hebrews 3:12-14)

In other words, having just reminded his readers of the ancient Jews who fell away from God and lost their salvation, he warns Christians not to do the same. He then draws further parallels with the Israelites who fell from grace and missed out on salvation:

"As has just been said: 'Today, if you hear his voice, do not harden your hearts as you did in the rebellion.' Who were they who heard and rebelled? Were they not all those Moses led out of Egypt? And with whom was he angry for forty years? Was it not with those who sinned, whose bodies perished in the wilderness? And to whom did God swear that they would never enter his rest if not to those who disobeyed? So we see that they were not able to enter, because of their unbelief." (Hebrews 3:15-19)

Can you see his line of reasoning? Can you follow his argument? Just as some of God's own people in the past lost their salvation through serious disobedience, so can we.

And do you notice whom he is writing to: *"brothers and sisters" (verse 12).* This passage, and indeed the whole book of Hebrews, is addressed to the Christian church. It is Christians who are being warned here that continued disobedience can result in a loss of salvation. The writer then continues in the next verse:

"Therefore, since the promise of entering his rest still stands, let us be careful that none of you be found to have <u>fallen short</u> of it." (Hebrews 4:1)

He continues this theme in the verses that follow, reminding his Christian brothers and sisters that:

"those who formerly had the good news proclaimed to them did not go in because of their disobedience." (Hebrews 4:6)

The book of Hebrews continues to warn Christians of the seriousness of sin and the danger of falling away, culminating in the dire and dreadful warning of chapter 6, that we previously quoted:

"It is impossible for those who have once been enlightened, who have tasted the heavenly gift, who have shared in the Holy Spirit, who have tasted the goodness of the word of God and the powers of the coming age and who have fallen away, to be brought back to repentance. To their loss they are crucifying the Son of God all over again and subjecting him to public disgrace." (Hebrews 6:4-6)

These first six chapters of Hebrews could not be clearer in warning Christians of the danger, indeed the very real possibility, of falling away and losing one's salvation.

The book of Revelation also contains dire warnings of the possibility of Christians having their salvation taken from them because of their continued disobedience to Christ. In Revelation chapters 20 and 21, we are told that only those whose names are written in the Lamb's Book of Life will escape the flames of hell and enter heaven. With that in mind, we turn to the early chapters of Revelation and discover something shocking: there will be people who initially have their names written in that book but, because of ongoing disobedience to Christ, their names will be *erased* from that book! They will lose their salvation! To the Christians in the church at Sardis, Christ says:

"Wake up! Strengthen what remains and is about to die! For I have found your deeds unsatisfactory in the sight of my God. Remember, therefore, what you received in the beginning; hold fast to it and repent! But if you do not wake up, I will come like a thief ...Those who are victorious I will not blot out their names from the book of life." (Revelation 3:2-6)

The inference is abundantly clear! Those who persist in disobedience will have their names blotted out of the book of life. They will lose their salvation.

Another dire warning is found in the preceding chapter. Jesus is addressing Christians in the church at Ephesus, and he warns them to repent of their sins or he will remove his presence from them:

*"Consider how far you have fallen! **Repent** and do the things you did at first. If you do not **repent**, I will come to you and remove your lamp stand from its place." (Revelation 2:4-5)*

Let us be clear about the symbolism being used here. The lamp stand represents the presence of Christ within the church. Revelation chapter 1 has already defined this. In that chapter, John was given a vision of seven golden lamp stands, one representing each of the seven churches that would be addressed in chapters 2 and 3. In John's vision, he saw Christ walking among the seven golden lamp stands, and in verse 20 he was told, *"the seven lamp stands are the seven churches"*. This is important. In threatening to remove his lamp stand from the church at Ephesus, he is threatening to remove his very presence from them. In other words, they would no long be his church. They would lose their salvation. And what prompted this dire warning? Their ongoing sin. Their lack of genuine repentance.

CONCLUSION

The weight of scripture is overwhelming. Salvation is not something that we own for life: it is something that we must walk in daily. Faith and repentance is not a single use coin, that purchases a lifetime membership in "Club Salvation". It's not a one-off payment, after which we can put our feet up and relax, living however we like. Christ demands that we follow him, not just for one day or one year, but for life. He calls us to submit to his Lordship, not just initially, but for the whole of our lives. Faith and repentance must be our daily response to Christ. We must live at the foot of the cross, daily trusting in him and throwing ourselves upon his mercy, seeking his forgiveness and pledging ourselves anew to follow him.

This might not be the assurance we would like to hear. It would be nice if there was a Bible verse that said, *"Once you have said the sinners prayer, you are saved forever",* but there isn't. Instead the scriptures say that you are saved:

"provided you continue in his kindness. Otherwise, you also will be cut off." (Romans 11:22).

The scriptures declare that:

"We have come to share in Christ, if indeed we hold our original conviction firmly to the very end." (Hebrews 3:14)

And Jesus said:

"The one who endures to the end will be saved." (Matthew 24:13)

NOTES

11. What Are We Saved From?

1. Robert Schuller "Dr. Schuller Comments," (letter to the editor), Christianity Today, October 5, 1984, pp. 12-13

13. How Are We Saved?

1. Rick Warren, "The Purpose Driven Life", p.74.
2. John Macarthur, "Apostates Be Warned: Part 2", on his "Grace To You" website, (gty.org).
3. J.I. Packer, in his Introduction to John Owen's book, "The Death of Death in the Death of Christ". See the Appendix for the full text.

14. What Are We Saved To?

1. Extract from: Among Gods Giants, The Puritan Vision of the Christian Life. by J.I. Packer. Introduction to Chapter 8
2. Extract from: Among Gods Giants, The Puritan Vision of the Christian Life. by J.I. Packer. Introduction to Chapter 8
3. Jim Reiher, The Eye of the Needle, 2016

15. The Curse Of The Shallow Sermon

1. Quoted in the article, "Willow Creek Repents?" on Christianitytoday.com
2. John MacArthur, in an interview with Phil Johnson, in his Grace To You broadcast on gtv.org, entitled, "The Church Growth Movement"
3. Quoted in the article, "Willow Creek Repents?" on Christianitytoday.com

OTHER TITLES BY KEVIN SIMINGTON

THE LITTLE BOOK OF CHURCH LEADERSHIP

"*The Little Book of Church Leadership*" is a little book with BIG ideas.

There is a crisis of leadership within the modern church. Not an *absence* of leadership. The modern church has plenty of leadership; just not the right sort. The kind of leadership that has evolved in many churches today is a long way from the leadership that was taught in the New Testament and practised by the first century church. Many churches have absorbed a philosophy and style of leadership that is more attuned to the business world than to the Bible. This book is a call to seriously re-evaluate the church leadership style that has developed in recent years and return to the patterns and principles of church leadership as outlined in the New Testament.

"*The Little Book of Church Leadership*" is available in print or as an eBook from SmartFaith.net, Amazon and all major online retailers.

FINDING GOD WHEN HE SEEMS TO BE HIDING

"*Finding God When He Seems to Be Hiding*" provides intelligent answers to the common questions and objections that are often roadblocks in people's journey towards faith. If God exists, why is there so much suffering in the world? What about all the killing in the Bible? How can a loving God send people to hell? Is the Bible reliable? What evidence is there for the resurrection of Jesus? What about evolution? Hasn't science and evolution disproved the existence of God? How can God permit abuse and religious violence?

This book addresses these and other common questions with remarkable clarity and provides answers that move beyond the standard, glib responses that are often proposed.

"*Finding God When He Seems To Be Hiding*" is available in print or as an eBook from SmartFaith.net, Amazon and all major online retailers.

MAKING SENSE OF THE BIBLE

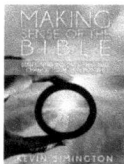

This book will change the way you read the Bible!

"Making Sense of the Bible" is a comprehensive guide to understanding and interpreting the Bible. It explores the remarkable journey of the Bible, from original text to modern translation, and will assist you to develop a more mature, complex understanding of the nature of its divine inspiration. It examines the many complex cultural and contextual issues that are essential in order to accurately apply the Bible's message. These include the difference between the two covenants, the nature of progressive revelation, the pre-Christian context of the Old Testament, and the necessity to read the whole Bible "Christologically" - through the lens of Christ's person and work.

What sets *"Making Sense Of The Bible"* apart from similar books is its intensely practical nature. Commonly misinterpreted doctrines are explored in detail, and important principles of interpretation are applied. A large range of key biblical doctrines are examined in detail.

This book is a must for ordinary Bible readers and serious students alike!

"*Making sense of the Bible*" is available in print or as an eBook from SmartFaith.net, Amazon and all major online retailers.

NO MORE MONKEY BUSINESS:

EVOLUTION IN CRISIS

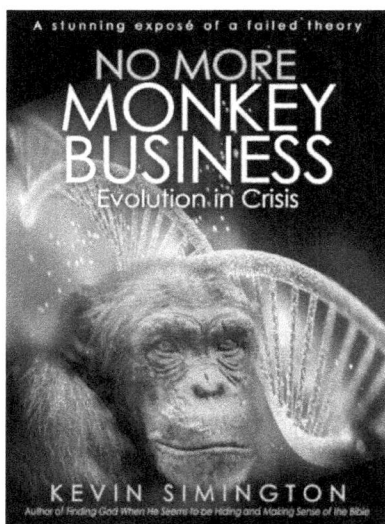

"*No More Monkey Business*" is a concise, easy-to-read summary of the overwhelming and rapidly accumulating scientific evidence against evolution. Written with wit, and using simple layman's language, yet brimming with incontestable scientific evidence, this book highlights the huge problems now facing Darwin's original theory. Each chapter is full of fascinating scientific facts and discoveries which now directly contradict Darwin's naïvely simplistic theory proposed more than a century ago. *"No More Monkey Business"* documents the abandonment of the theory of evolution by a growing tide of the world's leading scientists, as well as the startling declaration by several recent scientific conferences that the theory of evolution can no longer be considered to be scientifically tenable. This book will challenge those who have unthinkingly assumed evolution to be a proven fact and will enable Christians to defend their faith with confidence.

"No More Monkey Business" is available in print or as an eBook from SmartFaith.net, Amazon and all major online retailers.

THE STARPATH SERIES

A science fiction adventure series that is consistently receiving 5-star reviews around the world!

A dying world.
A desperate mission.
An unlikely hero.

"Incredibly well written, intelligent science fiction, by an author who really knows how to tell a story."

"I was hooked from the first page. The story is gripping and moves at a cracking pace. I also loved that there was humour and romance as well as edge-of-your-seat drama."

Available from: kevinsimington.com and Amazon

CONNECT WITH KEVIN SIMINGTON

Non-Fiction books and resources: smartfaith.net

Fiction books: kevinsimington.com

Facebook: https://www.facebook.com/ReflectionsKev/

ABOUT THE AUTHOR

Kevin Simington is a theologian and apologist who is passionate about helping Christians grow deeper in their faith. He spent 31 years in Christian ministry, as a church pastor and a Christian educator. He is now a full time author and speaker. His website, SmartFaith.net, and Facebook page, "Reflections on Faith and Life", provide valuable resources for defending the Christian faith and equipping Christians. Kevin's weekly blog, available through his website and Facebook page, provides incisive commentary on social issues, theology, apologetics and ethics, and is read by thousands of people worldwide. He also writes for "My Christian Daily", an international Christian magazine.